PROLOGUE

Hindsight has twenty-twenty vision. I cannot change what happened, nor will my narrative in any way attempt to whitewash or photo-shop any past indiscretions or exaggerate my achievements. God created this creature I call *self* to which my parents instilled core values. Confronting challenges head-on and accepting gifted opportunities have developed my personhood. I am a showgirl, glamour supported by depth of character.

By position of the stars at my birth or coincidence, traits attributed to a Gemini woman—despising boredom and craving spontaneity—fit my personality. As a Gemini, I am creative, emotionally nurturing, warm, and compassionate. However, I exercise control over my destiny. Life happens, but I make choices.

I know what it means to face the eye of a tiger—literally. On stage, a performing white tiger broke loose from his handler, Roy Horn, and sauntered toward me assessing what could have been his next meal. Lucky for me, he preferred prime beefsteak from Siegfried and Roy's refrigerator, but even a cat might crave some variety in his diet.

The girl next to me whispered, "Just stay perfectly still," and then she followed the others off stage. Thanks a lot. Keeping the cat in my periphery, I held my position and stared straight ahead, my mother's voice, *stay calm, think it through, and react with caution*.

The cat strode off stage. The band picked up and the girls sidestepped back into view, as if leaving stage were part of their routine. Since this was a rehearsal, no audience had been asked to choose between the lady and the tiger.

Mother's voice in my head might have prevented an abrupt end to my career before it began the summer of 1982. Edged off the road by a semi, I kept my cool, eased my Volkswagen *Bug* off the shoulder and down the ravine, preventing a rollover according to the California Highway Patrol report.

A quiet *thank you, Mom* with a continuing down the road toward my destiny.

A few years later, I discovered another side of my mother after I turned down an offer to dance in *Moulin Rouge* at the Las Vegas Hilton, second most extravagant show to *Jubilee* at the MGM Grand. When she asked why, I responded, "I can't go topless."

"You should have said 'yes.'" What a hoot! My religious but pragmatic mother had shown her true colors. She understood the Las Vegas score.

Released from that part of my Christian-planted inhibition, I agreed to dance bare breasted but made a pact with myself never to sleep my way into a production, a red line often tested, never crossed.

Hindsight may not change anything, but it instructs. Throughout my career, I considered *yesterday's experience* vital when making *today's decision*. Reconstructing my career history for this narrative forced me to dig deep into my yesterdays, not always pleasant. The process reinforced my personal assets, no great discovery. A successful career speaks well of how I presented myself when opportunities occurred. The frightening part, these same assets had been my greatest liabilities, and they left me vulnerable.

Two high school experiences illustrate my point. During my freshman year, I participated in cheerleading, basketball, and track, and my biggest passion outside of school, dance lessons. Sophomore and junior years I focused on academics, track, and dance. As a senior, I wanted cheerleading back in my schedule. Back then, boys performed and girls cheered.

My mother said, "You're setting yourself up for disappointment. Two hundred girls are competing for six positions, some with two or three years of experience."

"Mom, I can do it. I have a plan."

In addition to soft-landing roundups and cartwheels, I stuck out and shook my bootie, directing my caboose toward the boys on the team. They whooped and hollered and voted me in. I felt a surge of ecstasy, like hearing oohs and aahs from the audience five years later while performing in *Jubilee*. Through proper guidance and serious practice, my body had become a vehicle of artistic expression, and, I discovered, a tool of persuasion at a baser self-serving level. Oddly enough, I had yet to associate this new-found power as a means of sexual arousal. Not even on the level of flirting, like some of the girls seeking attention from boys by acting poor-helpless-me. I did not need a boy to carry my books to class; I had poise enough to sashay down the hall with every book from my locker balanced on my head.

The second high school experience to illustrate my vulnerability occurred on the beach at South Padre Island. Stephen Shultz, my steady boyfriend of two years, invited me to accompany his parents on their family vacation. We wandered off to a secluded area of the beach, when our ardor turned into a disagreement and he stomped off. Through tears, I heard a male voice heavily accented with Mexican inflections.

"Your boyfriend ran off and left you. So sad."

A split-second burst of anger delayed my sense of danger and gave this bedraggled beach bum an advantage.

He grabbed my arm and pulled my face down to his. "Maybe me and you should smoke a joint."

Straggly whiskers on puffy cheeks curved into a hideous smile, and squinty eyes glared. The image still haunts me.

"Let me go!" I yelled.

"Forget about your friend. I can make you feel real good." He tossed his head back as if tasting that good feeling.

I screamed, jerked my arm free, and sprinted, losing footing in the soft sand. A second man appeared and joined in the chase. I ran toward the ocean for better traction on the wet sand. My panic called up a level of strength never experienced before. I ran as if in a track event; no trophy, just my virtue, probably my sanity, and possibly my life.

Stephen, reconsidering our argument, had circled around the campsite and met me head on. I dropped to my knees exhausted. He would have been no match for the two men, but not wanting a witness, they retreated.

When we reported the incident to the beach patrol, the guy claimed a number of girls had been raped on that section of beach. He never bothered to investigate. I sensed negative vibes as he eyed my bare midriff between cut off t-shirt and shorts. He, not the two guys chasing me, prompted me to ditch them in the nearest trashcan back at the hotel.

My point with these two high school experiences, my assets—long legs and shapely body; poise and stature developed through dance, coupled with a Christian naivety ingrained as a child—gave me power but left me vulnerable. Throughout my career, I had to employ my assets to achieve in show biz, but superiors, peers, and outsiders often misread my intentions. Part of the problem was the culture of my chosen career, and partly the unique chemistry of my sexuality.

My red line offered no behavior guidelines to distinguish between sexual bantering and implicit sex for advantage. I knew my intention, but others sometimes misread my gregarious nature.

CHAPTER I

"Your mother should be leaving us today."

After the welling up in my chest subsided, I whispered, "I understand."

"She'll need your help to let go." Lisa floated her hand back and forth above the sheet palm down as if sensing vibes radiating from Mom. "She's determined to remain with us. A Taurus, if I recall."

A sob blended into a chuckle. "She's a stubborn woman."

"I first met your Mom the night she came to see us dance in *Jubilee*. Our going topless didn't bother her. She was very proud of you." My colleague over the last twenty-five years had found my soft spot. "Just last year she raved about your come-back performance in *Sassy* at the Starbright Theatre."

"Mom still lived with my son, André, and me. Together we took good care of her." My rising anger overcame my sorrow. "Just look at her now." I lowered my voice to a whisper. "Did you see all her bed sores?"

"I'm more peace therapist than aide, but I can tell she's experienced some neglect. Usually the patients from Advanced Health Care are free of skin infections."

I nodded, too choked up to correct her. I wanted to tell Lisa about every bad thing that happened since Mom broke her hip, the two-and-a-half hour surgery and her remarkable recovery in rehab, but Caroline would not let me take her back to my home. I agreed with my sister, not because she is a famous doctor, but I couldn't be at Mom's bedside day and night. Medicare would sooner put a patient in an expensive facility than offer more than a few hours per week assistance for a home aide.

My jaw tightened. "At that *place* before Advanced Health Care! *The premier assisted living facility of Las Vegas*, according to the woman at the Medicare office. Within a week, I knew Mom had to be moved"

Lisa backed from Mom's bed. "I know which place you're referring to."

I had found a willing ear and didn't let her escape. "Seldom any showers or clean sheets, food put in front of her with no encouragement to eat, the still-covered dish taken away. I brought a protein drink from my gym, but their policy would not allow me to feed it to her. And to top it off, they refused to release her when a bed opened up at Advanced Health Care, until I pitched an unholy fit."

"You did what was right."

"If only she had started her recovery there. Maybe we could have her home by now. The surgery went well. I stood alongside the technician at Mountainview Hospital who took her x-ray."

"A broken hip is the most difficult injury for an elderly patient to overcome emotionally." Lisa echoed Mother's point after she fractured her ankle. *When my hip breaks, my life will be over.*

"Your mom's body..." I flinched at hearing *body*, as if Mom was already dead, "...has mostly let go, but some areas near her abdomen refuse to budge." Her hand fluttered above the sheet around Mom's stomach area, this time like a final powder puffing before the curtain opens.

Lisa pressed my outstretched hand between hers, and I realized I, too, had been testing Mom's midsection for vibes. "You need to be alone with her. Please help her move on to her next life." She smiled, brushed my cheek, and released the tears my anger had been blocking. "I'll be in the office down the hall." A sympathetic gaze into my eyes, and she tiptoed out the door.

What might keep me from moving on when my time comes? My children! I called my sons Nicholas, André, and their dad, Scott. I called Caroline and our three half-siblings who shared our mother. I gave each a turn to say their goodbyes and give Betty Jeanne Peterson permission to leave this world. They mostly reminded Mom about good times in the past and that we would be together as a family in a couple weeks for Christmas. They hadn't accepted the reality of the holidays without her. She couldn't understand a word they said, probably recognizing the sounds of their voices.

A doctor in a white jacket with a name I couldn't pronounce appeared out of nowhere. Eyes glued to Mom's chart, she said half to herself, "There is nothing we can do for this one." She glanced up and blurted, "Oh, it's you again."

We had locked horns two care facilities ago. After I won the battle to have my mother transferred, I defied her order to leave the room while aides prepared Mom to be transported. I pointed out the discolored gown and sheets from her open soars. I'm a tiger when someone is hurting my Mom, or any one that I love.

I spoke through clenched teeth. "You are responsible for—"

The woman wagged a finger. "You need to calm down."

I glared at her and took a deep breath. In a soft but stern voice, I said, "How would you feel if that happened to your mother?"

"My mother is deceased. You need to get over this."

I glared. "Apparently some cultures handle grief differently?" Sarcastic, but I was upset.

ROGER STORKAMP & MIKEL PETERSON

"Mikel." Lisa had returned. "Please don't take your anger out on us. We're here to help your mother move on."

"Sorry, for that catty remark." Showgirls tend to get snotty, part of an aloof atmosphere. Lisa and I always tried to avoid acting that way.

She said, "You needn't apologize. I understand how you feel."

The other woman snorted and left the room.

"Has your mom loosened her hold on this life?"

I pointed to my cell phone. "I had her—our—family talk to her, but they mostly tried to lift her spirits, to give her hope."

"And you...?"

"I want to take her home with me where she belongs. She lived with us. My teenaged son found her lying on the floor in the bathroom and put her back to bed. She didn't want André to tell me she had fallen. They always shared little secrets and would giggle when I suspected something. He did the right thing, because she had broken her hip."

My voice cracked and I couldn't control my sniffles.

"André loved his grandmother."

"And she loves him. And his older brother, Nicholas, does too." I dabbed my nose with tissue. "Always afraid I'd send her to a retirement home. That's what she feared most, a place with just old people."

"You kept her with you as long as you could."

"Until she broke her hip. After fracturing her ankle, I continued to take care of her at home. Her mind was fading. Returning from aftercare, she didn't even recognize our house. Six years with us, and she couldn't remember where she lived."

Lisa gave an understanding nod and left the room. I touched Mom's cheek. "What must you be thinking now? That I pushed you out?"

Then it struck me, I was the daughter holding her back. I could not tell her to leave. I dipped the small sponge-on-a-stick into her glass of water and pressed a drop into her mouth. I repeated the process until she closed her lips on the sponge. I had received her final hug.

My boys and their dad arrived, Scott hesitating at the door to give my boys a moment with their grandma and me. His consideration for our feelings was part of the reason I loved him. Nicholas and André hugged me and stared at their grandma.

Mom's voice in my head: *Go. Your students are depending on you.* She had been proud that I never missed teaching my class or any scheduled stage performance. I felt her permission to leave.

Scott approached, glanced from Mom to me, and then accepted my embrace. I said, "Now that you're here, I can leave to teach my dance class." I glanced down at Mom. "You have to hold on until I get back."

"You're leaving?" André asked.

"Grandma wouldn't want me to disappoint my students or their parents."

"I think she wants you here." His voice pleading. "I want you to stay."

Nicholas said, "We'll be here, Mom. You can go."

"Thank you," Nicholas. I faced André. "Dad and your brother will be with you. Love you forever."

I rushed to the parking lot and got into my red Camaro—my last vestige of show biz—and checked my watch. Twenty minutes, plenty of time. I entered the flow of traffic and allowed my mind its freedom to reflect...

CHAPTER 2

"Mom, Jim. I decided I'm not going to college." I paused for them to digest my decision. "I'm going to be a professional dancer." Disappointment etched on her face and possibly embarrassment having this conversation in front of our dinner guest. "Two daughters in college at the same time would put too much of a financial burden on you."

Jim said, "That leaves nothing to fall back on. What if a career in dancing doesn't pan out? What would you have for a plan 'B'?" He glanced from Mom to me and then down at the napkin, its corner still tucked into his shirt. "Michelle could consider taking night classes. I might be able to finagle some scholarship money through a program at work."

His resources amazed us. An engineer at the Air Force Research Laboratory at Kirtland Military Base without a family of his own, Jim Mesnard adopted us. Neither Mom nor he ever expressed interest in his moving in to replace Dad as head of the household. Mom single-handed fulfilled that role since Don Lesmen Jr. moved out to become our *Texas Dad*. Grandpa Barker already held the title, *Texas Papa*.

"That's a very kind offer, but I need dance lessons, not college courses." I discovered my passion when Mom enrolled me in preschool dance classes. My love of animals could have steered me toward veterinary medicine, the only other career choice I seriously considered; a private investigator still just a fantasy.

"I could help out some with the cost." Jim already contributed financial assistance with Caroline attending Abilene Christian College in Texas.

"Dance lessons at a professional studio would require more than just a Band Aid." We laughed at the memory, and the tension in the room relaxed. Back in third grade—golly, Jim had been with us a long time—I stubbed my toe, tore loose the toenail and bled like a stuck hog according to Caroline. Blood and gore never bothered her, probably why she became a doctor. Jim came to my rescue with a Band Aid, and my family's relationship with him had begun. "You're already helping Mom with car payments."

Mom's turn to lower her eyes. She had given Caroline the family car, a new Honda Prelude, to take to college, tuition and most living expense covered by her scholarship. A used Volkswagen Beetle that I had dibs on replaced the family car. My boyfriend, Stephen Shultz, helped me paint it a passionate burgundy to match his Beetle.

"I want to strike out on my own. I'm ready to live away from home."

Face scrunched, Mom about to start sobbing again, a common occurrence because her baby daughter prepared to graduate and move away from home. "But you'll need career plans for your future. Your brothers and sisters have good solid jobs, and Caroline is on her way to one."

"I'll take a chance at a dancing career. In Hollywood."

"Hollywood, California?" Her about-to-cry expression wiped away by a gasp.

Jeyette Sparlin, dance teacher/mentor, stay with me as I face my mother. "In the counselor's office at school, I found a dance studio in North Hollywood. That must be right next to Hollywood."

"Yes, I know, Honey." Mom at her persuasive best while her eyes said *we'd talk later*.

I held my ground. "You doubted that I could make cheerleader my senior year."

"Yes, you did prove me wrong that time." She strung the words as if difficult to utter.

Resistance starting to thaw? "I can be successful this time, too."

"I'm sure you could, but California? Why not something here in Albuquerque or San Antonio, maybe Phoenix or even Denver? I don't want to lose sleep at night wondering what's happening to you out there."

"Mom, I'm only experimenting with a career, just like auditioning for a part in a school play. I'm not leaving home for good." Who was I fooling? This decision would be my rite of passage, and we both knew it.

"Where would she eat? Sleep?" Practical Jim. He faced me, "How would you get there?"

"I'd take my *Bug*," the intended graduation gift.

"The Bug?"

The Bug? Had Mom forgotten she agreed to give it to me? She usually called it *The Volkswagen*, as if it was Marilyn Monroe's Cadillac. "Where would you stay?"

"With Bonnie Murray's daughter, Tyler." My parents had come to terms with their separation early on, but my fascination with Dad's most recent partner may have touched off a tiny bit of jealousy. I considered both women beautiful, Mom of the Elizabeth Taylor sort and Bonnie more like Raquel Welch.

I held eye contact. "Bonnie said Tyler would welcome me into their home until I get on my feet. I'd get a waitressing job and check out dance studios, starting Dupree Dance Academy." I eyed the dishes ready to be cleared from the table and considered the dessert still in the kitchen. Serving meals had been my job, even when my brothers and sisters came with their families.

"With Tyler..." Mom flicked an eyelash as if brushing off a speck of lint. "Tyler and her partner?"

"Yes, Mom, Tyler Murray and Camila Griggs."

After visiting the middle-aged couple during spring break, Caroline decided to *come out of the closet* just with Mom and me. I had known since we were kids, because she and I played with different toys and different playmates, same sex for me and opposite sex for her. Puberty dictated we redirect our relationships toward courting and dating—me with a classmate at the freshman prom, and Caroline casually dating male friends from childhood. It didn't work for her.

Mom probably knew and maybe even felt relieved no longer having to doubt the fact. She taught us never to judge people based on their differences. She had felt the sting of a religious bias from her parents by marrying a Catholic, divorcing, and taking up with another Catholic. We had never discussed the topic of sexual preferences in our house, but Mom readily included it with other biases to be avoided.

I felt bad about my sassy attitude but continued my practiced speech. "Tyler sings in lounges and on harbor cruises. She recorded her own CD and earned a bit part in the TV series, *Night Rider* with David Hasselhoff. Camila won a major supporting role as Joy Paschal in *Force Vengeance* with Chuck Norris."

"Singing and acting. I don't believe they can help your dancing career." Mom had recovered her composure.

My need to apologize evaporated. "I could get a part in movies like *Grease* and *Fame*."

Mom's face screwed into a question mark. "How would you do that?"

"Through the Dupree Dance Academy. I'm sure there are others."

"We'll see when the time comes."

Happening in three months. For the moment, I decided not to push. Mom will come around. She raised me to be independent, and she will respect my dream.

Mom rose from the table. "I'll get our desserts."

Hey, that was my job. My role in the family evaporated, went *puff*, but Mom had prepared me for this moment since I was a child.

***

After Dad left us, Mom, quit her nursing job and devoted full time to raising Caroline and me, our older siblings lived elsewhere. We became *The Three Musketeers*, Mom driving us to track events, Caroline as a runner and I ran and jumped.

We lived in subsidized housing, where kids never participated in track events. I improvised a starting block by digging a trench in the dirt, lined up the girls in my sixth grade class, and demonstrated how to plant their feet and position body weight. We sprinted.

When Madison Middle School sponsored a turkey trot, I wasn't as cooperative. *Win that turkey for our Thanksgiving table* dominated my thoughts. Focusing on a goal, I became very competitive. Since that turkey incident, I obtained every job I auditioned for throughout my entire career, a very satisfying lifetime accomplishment. Proud humility, my virtue and my vice.

I was nine years old when Olga Korbut stunned the world with her gymnastic performance during the 1972 Olympics in Munich, Germany. I could do that, but my legs kept growing. I would earn a medal in the long jump, and my sister would certainly take the gold in the 400-meter relay. By junior high, I combined my jumping ability with modern dance classes taken since I was five. When Nadia Comaneci earned a perfect score in gymnastics at the 1976 Olympics in Montreal, Canada, I lost interest. Except with ice-skating, dance wasn't an Olympic event, and I couldn't skate.

Wrong on two accounts. I had to demonstrate my skills on ice to qualify as a showgirl in Las Vegas, and I danced my way to the 1984 Olympics in Los Angeles and again in the 1988 Pre-Olympics in Seoul, Korea.

My sister and I competed throughout high school and joined summer camps to improve our skills, Caroline's exclusively athletic, mine a combination of physical and artistic endeavor. I joined school clubs in areas of music and drama. My orchestra teacher pulled me aside to explain in blunt language that I hadn't an ear for music. If his goal had been to get me to drop out, he understood nothing about me. From then on, I slept with my violin! Almost. It occupied my nightstand where a few bow swipes across the strings accompanied my morning prayers.

My sister suffered the same indignity when she first tried out for basketball. Her freshman coach said, "You're tall, but you don't have the speed and agility to be a ball handler."

Caroline proved her wrong, lettering in track and playing varsity basketball in her junior and senior years. She received a full-ride basketball scholarship to Abilene Christian University. Today, Dr. Caroline Peterson is a nationally renowned OB/GYN specialist with honor-roll-status at Health Grades Professional Evaluation Board. She lives in Dayton, Ohio, with her partner, Cindy Schaffer. My sister is still my best friend.

High school drama and theater taught me confidence and empathy. I could make people laugh with silly routines. One assignment was to select a poem and deliver it to the class. In a child-like voice, I recited:

Fishy, fishy, in a brook
Daddy caught it on a hook
Mommy fried it in a pan
Daddy ate it like a man.

The kids loved it but my teacher thought it childish. Lesson learned, the audience gets to decide if a performance works or not. Smiles my antics brought to the faces of special education classes gave me goose bumps. Today in my children's dance classes, I assign simple routines for a less capable child to experience success.

I loved school and seldom missed a day through sickness, never by skipping like some of my friends. At my high school reunion, classmates prepared a display of postcards, placemats, and other promotional items with my photograph attached. I wowed my ex-classmates with the picture of me in showgirl costume holding my infant son, and promised to pose for the camera holding my grandchild when or if he or she arrives.

CHAPTER 3

My mother was an accomplished woman; nurse, volunteer, pilot, and mother of seven, each role unique yet fulfilled. She and her husband, Dr. Joseph Peterson, ran the osteopathic hospital in Albuquerque, a practice Dr. Peterson started in a building erected by Betty Jeanne's father, our *Texas Papa*. He introduced his daughter to Dr. Peterson during the hospital's construction, but they didn't become involved until my mother graduated.

On their first date, Dr. Peterson stopped to check on a pregnant Hispanic woman in Old Town Albuquerque, not yet the tourist destination it is today.

He returned to my mom waiting in the car. "The woman is about to give birth. Please come in the house and assist." Just before entering the dirt-floor kitchen, he warned, "They'll offer food, but don't eat or drink anything not piping hot."

Both accomplished private pilots—Mom, the first female to solo in Albuquerque—they flew their Cessna to small villages in Mexico delivering medical supplies and offering free care to the underserved. She presided over the Doctors' Wives Association raising revenue to develop scholarships for medical students and for supporting young doctors going into practice. She raised six children to adulthood; Gary Peterson, a Viet Nam vet with an airline career in Texas, Pamela Peterson, a teacher in New Mexico, Suzanne Peterson, a career in Aero Space Engineering, and Jeff Peterson who died without having achieved his dream of playing professional baseball, my sister Caroline Peterson, OB/GYN specialist, and me, dancer/showgirl/mom.

What brings such a high profile glamorous couple with a seemingly compatible marriage to the point of divorce? Perhaps Dr. Peterson's later-in-life surge of guilt over a previous divorce, that marriage never granted a papal annulment. I can only guess, yet be thankful for the hand of fate that brought Caroline and me into existence.

Mom experienced painful losses, being dropped from the social register with professional, political, and business leaders. No more brushing shoulders with the Maloof family, who chartered the First National Bank later merged with Wells Fargo. From his collection of celebrities' cars, Phil Maloof had loaned Mom Marilyn Monroe's Cadillac to drive around town. She lost the Cadillac, but Caroline and I were lulled to sleep nestled in Mom's arms while she rocked in a chair designed by Sam Maloof, the Maloof Lebanese family patriarch.

Our association with the Maloof family recurred when I experienced a high school crush on George Maloof. We had a dinner date and a great time together. Our paths crossed again in Las Vegas, but I never had a chance to perform at his Fiesta or Palms casinos.

Mom met my father, a dashing Hispanic musician, and she made a life changing decision. They never married creating an additional contention between her and Texas Papa Barker. Not only had she walked away from a stable marriage, Don Lesmen was a Hispanic and another Catholic. Caroline and I, including our older brothers and sisters, never quite measured up to Texas Papa's other grandchildren because we weren't Texans. Yet, I admire our grandfather. When *Mima*, my grandmother, was killed in a head-on car crash, friends and family encouraged him to sue the elderly couple in the other car.

"It was an accident!" End of story. An interesting anecdote; Texas Papa would drive around the streets of Quanah, Texas, every Sunday morning honking his horn, a strong reminder to get to church.

When our brother, Jeff, left home to live with relatives in Quanah, Mom joked, "I'm an empty nester with two fledglings."

She devoted full attention to Caroline and me, giving us our nicknames, Pobe and Shelly, probably from the TV show about a divorced mother raising two girls. Mom showed no favoritism, even dressing us alike as children despite our thirteen-month age difference. By high school, we had developed different personalities, Caroline older and more conforming to Mother's ideal, and I somewhat of a challenge, a *handful* Mom often said. I doubt she loved Caroline more than me, but my sister's career goals suited Mom better. Both her daughters exhibited high energy, one more focused, the other more *spread out*. I detest the word *scattered*. Curiosity and risk taking might better define my motivations.

I attempted to follow in Caroline's footsteps throughout high school, but with her six-foot-one-inch height, her stride exceeded mine. As a showgirl in *Jubilee*, I was classified a *short nude* barely over the five-foot-eight-inch minimum.

Where Caroline continued a career tradition on my mother's side, Dad and his family influenced my career choice. I love my dad, and I understand why he didn't follow through as a live-in parent when we were growing up. Mom paying more attention to their two daughters than to him coupled with his free spirit probably caused him to move on, but he chose to leave during an impressionable time in my life. With Jeffery gone to Texas, Gary off to Viet Nam, and Dad moving out of our house, I was losing all the adult males in my life. To top it off, Mom became stubborn—she is a Taurus—and wouldn't allow us much time with Dad's side of our family. If it hadn't been for our older sisters, Pam and Suzanne, we probably would have seen them but maybe once a year at Christmas.

Dad grew up in a bilingual household in Old Town Albuquerque. His parents sent him to St. Michael's Academy, a Catholic boarding school in Santa Fe all twelve years. His football team elected him captain, and he earned a championship medal in cross-country track and field.

"Cross country track and field?" I recently confronted Dad about his awards.

"Not an oval prepared surface like you and your sister trotted across, but through open country. Used to be an Olympic category before my time. Now cross-country pertains to skiing in the Winter Olympics. Too tough for a summer event."

After graduating from high school in 1945, Dad worked at their family market and played drums professionally in his father's musical group, Don Lesmen Band. Dad provided the background rhythm in Glen Campbell's Western Wrangler Group from 1958 until Glen left Albuquerque for California in1960 to become famous. Soon after, Dad moved in with Mom, an eleven-year-older divorced woman, a credit to Mom's vitality and charm.

Dad moved out when I was five, and he attended business school in Long Beach, California. In 1975, he relocated in Texas as a five-state factory representative for musical instruments. When Charles Brown came out of retirement to do a few gigs in lounges and some recordings, Dad performed as his drummer.

Fond memories of Old Town with my Lesmen family remain with me. Grandma Edna and her twin sister, Edith, sang duets in the old Spanish Mission, San Felipe de Neri, built in 1793. Grandpa and Grandma lived a couple blocks down the street at

524 Romero, their house not quite as old. They were very popular in the community, she being crowned *Queen of Old Town*.

Music seeped from every nook and cranny of that adobe brick building. Mom didn't feel welcome when Caroline and I visited Dad's parents, because Grandpa Lesmen couldn't forgive her for changing our legal name from Chavez to Peterson. He had no qualms about changing the family name from Chavez to Lesmen, *the man* in Spanish, so his band sounded less Hispanic, even though Great Grandma Chavez emigrated from Spain, not Mexico.

Grandpa said, "Gringos expect a *Chavez* band to strum guitars, not play saxophone."

The Lesmen adobe house still stands converted to the *Candy Lady*, a specialty sweets shop with an adult-only back room. God bless this Catholic home! On their web site, customers are required to declare that they are over eighteen before ordering an adult selection or even viewing the products. Among their offerings, nut clusters, vagina pops, and stand-up dark chocolate penises with a white chocolate drizzle. Recently, they produced a sugar replica of blue meth for the television series, *Breaking Bad*, a novelty item available at the front counter. Apparently, drugs are not as harmful to adolescents as explicit sex. Lesmen's Music Store thrives today at 5413 Lomas Blvd, Old Town Albuquerque, under the ownership of Mark and Polly Padilla.

Occasionally, Mom drove us to Texas to spend time with Texas Papa. Dad would stop by in his motor home and take us to his and Bonnie's ranch in DeKalb, Texas. I felt comfortable with Dad's new partner, she being the image I wanted for myself when I grew up, tall and stately with cream skin and long blond hair. She raised horses and rode like the wind.

My favorite mare for barrel racing foaled during one of our visits, and I witnessed the birthing process. The veterinary explained the step-by-step from the first observable signs in the mother's body to her umbilical cord breaking when her colt struggled to stand. That experience coupled with raising my poodle nudged me in the direction of an animal-centered career. Ultimately, I preferred humans to animals.

As an adult, I have become closer to my father, and when Mom passes, I might need him even more. Oozing with charm, as a female he would have been an ideal showgirl. Musically talented, he exuded glamour and class, and beautiful girls gravitated toward him, mostly tall blonds. My mother was brunet but definitely glamorous, and he fell head-over-heels for her. Unfortunately, Don Lesmen Jr. thrived on female attention, a crossover vulnerability I share with him, as Mom pointed out numerous times throughout my career.

I have nearly conquered that character flaw, Mom. I will keep you updated about my progress with relationships.

CHAPTER 4

Rites of passage to adulthood usually involve a journey of some sort, for Caroline well-planned incremental steps from college to career, for me a plunge head first into a canyon of possible outcomes eight hundred miles from home.

Planning my move to California, Mom nearly washed Los Angeles off the roadmap with her tears. We laughed at my silly joke, but her eyes watered every time we discussed my plans. I was her baby and she hated to see me leave. Anticipating the thrill of an adventure, I resisted the urge to break down and stay home.

The Bug, its official name for the time being, had been packed the previous day including the sewing machine Mom bought for my home-economics class. Left behind were my honors, medals, trophies, cheerleading uniform, and the scrapbook that my sister, Suzanne, helped me develop. The blank pages in my life's story would fill quickly. My bedroom remained as-is for Mom to play make-believe with her phantom daughter, Michelle, like the crying room in church for moms with babies.

On the passenger seat, patiently waiting for Mom and me to cry our goodbyes, sat my friend, Steve, I had invited along as a traveling companion. Not Stephen Shultz as Mom and Jim had assumed.

"You mean Stephen," Mom had corrected when I told her who agreed to ride shotgun, her final concession before allowing me to drive my *Bug* out west.

"No, not Stephen." I chose that moment to announce our break-up. "He and I agreed our career choices set us in separate directions." I began to sob and Mom hugged me, not letting go until I broke free.

"Did he…?"

"No, Mom, he didn't ditch me. We both think it is better this way." I doubt she believed me.

"Two years together and you're walking away?" Mom had envisioned turning her rambunctious unpredictable daughter over to a stable college graduate four years from now.

Some tough decisions seem more difficult when forced to admit them to family. Stephen and I had already cried our way into accepting our separation. We decided to seek our fortunes without being tied down. His parents took our decision even harder than Mom did.

Five AM on the last day of August, 1982, I kissed Mom one final time and hugged Jim—he made a lame excuse about needing to be at work early and our house just happened to be on the way.

In the long shadow of the Sandia Mountains, behind the wheel of *The Bug*, I set out to seek my fortune. As we cruised west on Interstate 40, our descending toward the Rio Grand River matched the rising of the sun, a frozen-in-time moment until we reached the bridge. The fully risen sun washed out the apricot-tinted sky from which Sandia Mountains earned their Spanish name. After we climbed out of the river basin toward the high plains of Arizona, a sun-scorched and desert-brown vista dominated.

The Petrified Forest was a disappointment; all the trees were lying down and broken into pieces, and the dinosaurs were just colorful roadside statues. The big hole made by a meteor ten thousand years ago near Winslow, Arizona, was impressive.

We were Martin Milner and George Maharis from the TV series, *Route 66*, my Dad's favorite show mainly because of the Corvette they drove. When I become successful, I will buy him that car, or one like it. Mom will get Marilyn Monroe's Cadillac back from her friend, Philip Maloof, and I will buy her an airplane. My Sister can purchase her own toys when she becomes a successful doctor. Only part three of my fantasy had come true.

At the Welcome-to-Kingman sign half way to our destination, I blurted, "I've been here before! With my three sisters."

Steve asked, "What were you doing here?"

"I'm not sure. Just a memory flashback of two VW Beetles, Caroline with Pam and her son Brad in one and Suzanne and me in the other. They spun out on ice and teetered over the edge of an embankment. We were on a road trip. That's all I recall."

"No chance of ice this time of the year." Steve scanned the map on his lap. "What motel are we staying at?"

"The El Trovatore Inn." I pulled onto Smiley Burnett Drive.

"Been there before?"

"Nope. Just saw the sign back a few miles advertising a Route 66 experience for less than five dollars a night." One room, two beds, and no hanky-panky. Maybe a little, but two separate beds. No way I was about to destroy our high school friendship. Tom Bodett had yet to leave a light on at any Motel 6 back in 1982. I took a picture to send to Mom, the first of thousands taken over the course of my career.

After basking on Malibu Beach and watching a few brave souls kite surfing, Steve and I parted, he to the airport and I on to Van Nuys where I gave *The Bug* a well-earned rest in front of a California style bungalow.

ROGER STORKAMP & MIKEL PETERSON

Tyler and Camila welcomed me with open arms and house rules. Nothing written or even suggested, just assumed when I entered their home. Neat as a pin, demanding it be kept that way, except by Tyler's seven other housemates who violated every rule I envisioned for myself. Yorkie puppies nestled on a pillow-bed in the front room, free to roam but mostly waiting to be hand-fed by their surrogate mom. I loved them, and I loved Tyler for her appreciation of animals. I might not miss Mimi, my poodle since grade school, as much as I feared.

I filled my tank with gas and gave the leftover money toward my rent. I intended to find a waitress job the next day.

CHAPTER 5

My third day since leaving home, I landed my first real job, Love's Barbeque in Hollywood. Throughout high school, I earned money by baby-sitting, house cleaning, taking on odd jobs, and cutting boys' hair without ever receiving a regular paycheck. That evening, I wrote one of many letters to Mom, because calling long-distance cost too much. Must save those precious minutes for important times like when I became homesick. Ha! With that plan, I would be on the phone every night, if it weren't for two wonderful women and seven yapping puppies. I kept busy during the day, each one a new adventure.

For me, waitressing was a natural fit with my skills and my career choice. High school athletics prepared the necessary stamina, and dance lessons instilled agility and charm. Food service was a fallback career many experienced performers utilized to pay the bills. Camila set the example for me. My role as family server back in Albuquerque made taking and delivering orders a breeze.

Near the end of my shift on that first day, Buddy Ebsen and his wife, Nancy Wolcott, chose seats in my section, an important enough event for me to make that long-distance call home. I remembered him from *Beverly Hillbillies* back when I was still in the womb, or I at least felt Mom's belly laugh when she watched it every Wednesday night on CBS. My earliest memories of comedy were reruns of Buddy as Jed Clampett and his television family. I was too young to understand the irony my mom felt. She experienced the reverse turn of events, moving from affluence to near poverty. I felt bad when the series ended, and I had the chance to scold Buddy for it.

"My mom is still mad at you." Buddy set down his menu, smiled at Nancy across the table, and faced me, pencil and pad in hand. I never chewed gum on the job.

"Why on earth would the mother of such a lovely young lady be angry with me?"

"You stopped making us laugh."

"Would you like me to tell some jokes 'til our barbeques get here?"

"I mean your TV show with Daisy and Grandma and Jethro."

"Remember the oil well that made the Clampett family rich?"

"Yes, that's why the story seemed so real." Mom explained it to us two girls in pink bunny pajamas snacking on carrots and hopping around the bed.

He chuckled. "The well stopped pumping oil."

"That was true! The oil well, I mean?" Of all the embarrassing things I've uttered over the years, that was one silly response I would like to take back.

"The show's oil well had been the ratings, and they moved on to stars like *Lucille Ball* and *Carol Burnett*.

I flinched at his blaming two of my favorite comedians for causing his show to fail, as if I had been responsible for the drop in ratings. I laughed at the craziness of *Beverly Hillbillies*, but female comedians represented performers I aspired to, even after committing my body and spirit to a dance career.

Buddy's acceptance of the inevitable put me at ease. "Now Nancy and I can sit back and enjoy Love's wonderful barbeque. How long have you been working here?"

"My first day, and it will be my last if I don't quit gabbing."

"We come here often. Nancy and I will vouch for your charm and efficiency." He glanced at the menu, even though he probably knew it by heart.

With my income secured, I scouted the dance studios starting with Roland Dupree Dance Academy in Hollywood. According to the brochure, his instructors had performed on stage, and in television and films. Since meeting Buddy Ebsen at Loves, I'd become star-starved, and Hollywood seemed the place to satisfy that desire. After a few trial classes, word spread among the students that Joe Tremaine, a former instructor at Dupree, recently started his own dance studio. *Joe Tremaine School of Dance, Studio of the Stars* at 308 Ventura Avenue, North Hollywood, shortened the commute from my apartment in Van Nuys.

Mr. Tremaine sold me on his program. "We are *the* studio of stars. Our connections with directors, producers, and production companies eliminate the cattle-call process of dance auditions."

I felt mixed emotions. In high school, the competition to prove myself was half the fun, although most of the anxiety. The next few months, I sweated through Joe Tremaine's own brand of heart pumping, high kicking, and funky-and-fun style of jazz dance made popular in the French Quarter of New Orleans, and loved every moment of it. *Ben Gay*, my only boyfriend at the time, had nightly access to every sore muscle in my body.

Girls in Tremaine's class outnumbered boys, a normal gender difference I had experienced in high school. An open attitude toward gays encouraged each male dancer, gay or not, to freely express himself. Joe Tremaine never flaunted his homosexuality,

33

but didn't hide it either. Most important, I had opposite-sex dance partners available for practice.

After a strenuous workout at either the studio or Love's Barbeque or both, warmth and comfort greeted me at Tyler and Camila's home. If they were away, I had the puppies all to myself. When our three schedules allowed, we would eat together, share highlights of school and jobs, and play games. Acting out *Charlie's Angels*, one of us would imitate Bill Murray's voice as the mysterious Bosley and set up our challenge. We would discuss our strategy and cover each other in dangerous situations, always winding up in a shootout. We switched roles, but my favorite was Cameron Diaz as Natalie Cook.

They supported my goal to be a dancer, even renamed *The Bug* as *Barysh* after Mikhail Baryshnikov from the Kirov Ballet in Russia. They set me up with Kate, their managing agent, to have my first professional headshot taken. When Caroline came to visit us, Kate did one for her too.

We shared our dreams about acting, singing, and dancing. I wish they had encouraged me to study in all three areas rather than concentrate on dance. As for Tyler's dream to raise a child, we joked that I was too old to qualify. Eventually, she gave birth to Austin through artificial insemination.

Cancer took Tyler from us in 2012, yet no one lived a healthier life than she did—an occasional dish of *Häagen-Dazs* Ice Cream, her only indiscretion. She blamed genetics for her illness. I believe in destiny. Tyler's funeral was beautiful, if one can describe a sad event that way. It was held on the cruise ship where she performed, her family and friends aboard to say *bon voyage*.

Mom's funeral—I struggled with the image—will be spectacular, but I refuse to say *good-bye*. She has been with me every step of the way in my life and my career. She will be with me even after she leaves us.

Financially and emotionally, I felt ready to move to my own studio apartment. My housemates insisted I wait until turning twenty-one, and Camila would help me get a job as cocktail server. She worked at The Daisy on Rodeo Drive in Beverly Hills where movie stars mingled with wealthy movers and shakers. Her coworker, Nichole Brown, met O.J. Simpson at The Daisy. Camila described the night he drove up in a new sports car, sauntered into the nightclub, and handed Nichole the keys with a birthday card. They planed to marry after O.J.'s divorce is finalized.

I grew more excited each morning, a day closer to my twenty-first birthday.

Once while shopping with Camila, we stopped at The Daisy to pick up her paycheck. The lounge had not yet opened for business, so I played *Let's Pretend*, a CBS radio show my older brothers and sisters listened to back in the fifties. Mom continued to play the game with Caroline and me. I imagined every seat in the place occupied by my favorite stars from movies and television. From the Agatha Christie movie *The Mirror Crack'd*, I placed Elizabeth Taylor across from Kim Novak. Along side them sat Rock Hudson and Tony Curtis. I marveled at how much my mother resembled Elizabeth Taylor in that movie.

Camila's voice broke the spell. "I'm ready, let's go."

At the door, I glanced back at a quiet booth in the corner and there I imagined Mom and Dad, the true heroes in my life.

Living with Tyler and Camila had been great, but I needed time alone to sort out my life. Mom would be available by phone when necessary, I could drive to Tyler and Camila's house, and I had a few friends at work and school. Time had come to take that next step toward independence.

Amenities stated in the apartment-for-lease advertisement consisted of an outdoor pool (incapable of holding water) a washing machine, the ring around its lid alternately embedded with mold and a chalky substance, and a two legged table hinged to the kitchen wall. As an add-on, one crazy neighbor at no extra charge. An older man with a large heart and belly was kind and helpful. After he walked in without knocking to introduce himself and offer advice about the neighborhood, I kept my doors locked at all times.

I slept on the floor until I made a futon bed with the sewing machine Mom bought for me. Fashioned from fabric over thick foam, it could function as a cozy couch for two very close friends. With a reverse folding, it laid flat with the backrest functioning as a pillow.

My studio apartment became home, and with careful budgeting, I paid the rent and utilities, bought food for myself and gas for *Barysh*, and had some cash left for dance lessons. Thankfully, Tremaine offered a pay-as-you-go plan. The few times I wrote home for money, Mom and Jim supported me.

Camila called me one Saturday afternoon, her voice a notch higher than usual. "You have to help me out. I'm due at work in one hour, and I'm stuck doing retakes at Universal Studios."

"What can I do?"

"Fill in for me. Okay?"

"I don't know anything about mixing drinks." Six months short of my twenty-first birthday didn't enter our conversation.

"The bartender does that, all you have to do is take orders." A thousand thoughts fogged my brain. "I know you can do it."

Her confidence cinched it. "What should I wear?"

"Black slacks and a white shirt. I keep an extra black bowtie in the break room. Tell you what, there is a limo guy half-asleep waiting for passengers that won't be released very soon. He'll pick you up within an hour and take you home at the end of your shift. The place doesn't close until two, and you shouldn't be driving alone at that hour."

I thought, *yes, Mother* but said, "I'll be ready."

I opened the door to a smiling face, dark moustache, and sparkling eyes.

"Your carriage is waiting."

A younger version of my father, having traded his Hispanic accent for a harsh Middle Eastern one beckoned. My shocked reaction didn't faze him.

"Camila Griggs sent me."

The sound of his voice intrigued me, different from most people in Albuquerque.

"Thank you, *James*. To The Daisy, please." I enjoyed the moment.

Limo Guy—I've mentally blocked his name—bowed, donned his cap, and opened the passenger door. "You get to ride up front with me."

He escorted me through the back door to The Daisy and grabbed a girl by the arm. "Tell Toots I brought her a good one."

An ancient yet beautiful movie-star-type, probably from the silent film era, scrutinized me up and down.

"She's not blond. You know I prefer blonds."

"Some times I'm blond." Like when I was a year old, maybe. This was the limit of dishonesty I allowed myself to achieve a goal.

"Can you pop the cork on a champagne bottle?"

"It's been a while." In a previous life, maybe.

"Just remember to twist the bottle and not the cork, and for God's sake, aim it away from the table." She wafted a hand in the direction of the lounge. "Okay, get out there. The girls will tell you which tables are yours." I took a couple of hesitant steps when I heard the dreaded question, "By the way, you are twenty one, aren't you?"

I said, "Yes, this is my twenty-first year." True, if you start counting from the day I was born.

Three o'clock in the morning, *Limo Guy* stood alongside his vehicle, door held open. I dragged my wretched body to the car and slid onto the passenger seat. "Thanks."

"It's what I do, haul celebrities around." I was about to protest when he added, "And when I'm lucky, a Debutante."

"Debutante?"

"A young woman of certain charm publically entering society. According to some of my earlier passengers, you made quit a splash in there." All the door locks clicked, and I struggled not to show any sign of fear. Camila would not send a killer or rapist.

At my apartment, I thanked him and tried to open the door."

"Hold on." The locks clicked open. "I'll pick you up the next time you get called to work."

"I have my own car, but thank you anyhow."

"Allow me the honor, at least for the time being. I'll be here an hour before check-in time."

"How will you know I need a ride?"

"It's part of my job to know. Try to be ready on time."

I must have done well that night because they offered me employment, but only on weekends. That didn't matter. I belonged at The Daisy. When I filled out their employee data sheet, I closed my eyes and made a tiny check in the box stating I was over twenty-one, an extension of the truth by a few months.

I had a better paying job, a friend with a limousine, and a chance to circulate among important people, Joe Tremaine Studio during the day and The Daisy on weekends.

One day after class, *Limo Guy* double-parked in front of Tremaine's studio.

"Here's my ride. See you tomorrow." I waved good-bye as the other girls stood in awe. Whispering, "Thanks," I stepped into the back seat, the door held open for me. I giggled. "Circle around and then drop me off at my car a couple of blocks ahead."

"I have other plans for us." He pulled away before I could object. "You're not working tonight and no one's at home to worry about you being late." Dark eyes appeared in the rear view mirror. "You do live alone, don't you?"

"An elderly gentleman looks out for me. He'll call my cousin if I get home too late." *A big mean cousin twice your size*, but I didn't feel threatened enough to extend my little white lie. My neighbor, Henry, had no notion that Tyler or Carmela existed. He just kept his nose in my business out of curiosity. Sometimes, I changed my routine just to drive him crazy.

I never considered time spent with *Limo Guy* as dating. Ten years my senior, we just hung around together. Still hurting from my separation with Stephen back home, I was not ready for a relationship, but I enjoyed having male companions. The male dancers at Tremaine's Studio were mostly gay, and they treated me like their sister.

"Where are you taking me?"

"Just beyond sight of those gawkers, and then you can move to the front seat where you belong." He parked not far from *Barysh*; I could have thanked him, jumped out, and driven off, but I slid onto the passenger seat.

"We're going to see *West Side Story*."

"Where?"

"At a hangout where some of us drivers spend time waiting for calls. We've rented the movie and the machine to play it on our TV."

Amongst those uniformed men, relaxed, backslapping, and talking smart before their shifts, I became Snow White with a few oversized dwarves.

On the way back to the studio to get *Barysh*, *Limo Guy* said, "You know that dancer in the movie, Loco, member of the Shark Gang? He's an instructor at Debbie Reynold's Dance Studio. His real name is Jaime Rogers."

I had saved that studio for last because of its reputation for tough, advanced lessons for which I might not have been ready. Watching Loco dance in *Westside Story*, he became my next challenge.

"I took the liberty to pick up an application for you." *Limo Guy* pulled an envelope out from his suit jacket. "Hope you don't mind." He winked. "If you send it to him right away, you might be in for a little surprise."

CHAPTER 6

My first day at Debbie Reynold's Dance Studio at 6514 Lankershim Blvd, North Hollywood, I arrived before the building opened. I parked *Barysh*, curious who would be my instructor, probably some understudy. Jaime might observe me dance as a final test.

When the janitor opened the door to shake a mop, I stepped up and said, "Hi, I'm a bit early, but I need to check on the dance schedule for Jaime's class." Another slight leeway from the truth, but never with my moral behavior.

He shrugged, "Suit yourself," as if anyone wanting to get in early was unusual and probably stupid.

He shoved the door full open and stepped aside. A blast of hot air burst forth heavy with an offensive odor. I've known smells of gym classes and how they differ from dance studios, but this was a unique combination. I glanced at the fellow still holding the door ready for me to bolt into fresh air, when I noticed his heavy perspiration. Glad he wasn't one of the dancers.

"It's kind of hot in here." I mentioned the obvious.

"Get used to it. Jaime keeps the heat on, even on hot summer days. Crazy, but I get to go home and take a shower when I'm done here."

Two discoveries: Jaime will probably be the instructor and conditions will be nearly intolerable, excessive heat with no windows to let in fresh air.

Slowly the students trickled in, each girl taking a spot alongside the Barres aligning all four walls, some nodding a *hello* but no one socializing. I selected an opening and heard my first attempt at conversation.

"That's Judy's spot."

"She got booted last night. Let the new girl have it."

Booted at night? I should have taken a cue from that.

Jaime approached from behind, unannounced by either him or any morning greetings from the students. Immediately the strange odor became apparent, cigarette and alcohol breath.

"You must be the new one."

An older girl who had been exercising near the exit door poised to block my escape, an-inside-my-head joke, reappeared at Jaime's side holding a clipboard. He glanced at my resume, but he didn't set down his morning cocktail or remove the cigarette dangling from his lips. I remained under the spell of a middle-aged Loco from the Sharks gang in *West Side Story* rather than an egotist locked into his past successes.

He spoke through a plume of smoke. "Here for the scholarship?"

I nodded as if I had known one was available. This could be my lucky break.

"Let's see if you can live up to...," he glanced back at my file. "Jeyette Sparlin's opinion of your ability."

Jeyette had been my high school dance instructor, the only name I could think of when filling out the application. Not wanting to burn my bridges, I hadn't asked Joe Tremaine for a recommendation. Jaime must have assumed I was right out of high school, which, I discovered later, probably made me a more attractive as being innocent and vulnerable. If talented, all the better. No doubt, he intended to ride me hard to make a point, and I welcomed his challenge.

He scrutinized my body, and I felt his gaze linger on my crotch.

"Trac, get her some knee pads," he yelled, as his assistant headed out the rear door. Not my crotch, but my knees held his attention, yet I could hardly keep them from knocking. Why knee protection? Were new students required to scrub the floor? Or worse?

Trac returned almost immediately handing me pads to pull up over my legs. I made believe I wore them often. The way she ran to his every demand, I sensed more than a student-instructor relationship between her and Jaime. Once I saw her dance, I didn't care if they slept together. I wanted to be as good as she was.

Three-and-a-half hours of Jumping, running, and doing knee slides, I no longer made fun of the pads. Jaime's training strategy was extremely hardcore. I had experienced competition already as a child and survived all that Hollywood could throw at me thus far. Here was my chance to demonstrate that I had what it takes.

The next morning, Jaime approached, Trac at his side with clipboard in hand.

"Mike." Smoke drifted from each nostril.

I meekly responded, "Mikel, Mike with an 'l' at the end"

"Whatever. You got the scholarship thanks to your long legs. Now if I can teach you to dance, we'll be in business." He glanced toward the rear door, and Trac obediently retreated.

Not my crotch or even my knees, but my legs. Why was I not surprised? Other than Trac, most of his girls were long-legged, many of us taller than him. However, he was still tough for his age. In a fit of disgust, he would set down his drink and physically demonstrate a difficult move. He would eyeball each of us and yell, "*Capish!*" With a name like *Jaime Juan*, I doubt he was Italian. If a girl continued with bad form, he would kick her legs from under her. I concentrated, never giving him cause to treat me that way.

43

Soon, I discovered the benefits of Trac's close relationship with Jaime—she got the auditions for dancing parts in movies like *Staying Alive* with John Travolta, but at a high price to my notion. I reconsidered my hard-set red line separating me from mentors or benefactors. If Trac and Jaime were a couple, why not form a working partnership? When I observed him interact with his other girls, I realized he was not in any committed relationship. My focus centered on my lessons, and I avoided social relationships with everyone, especially the instructor.

Only female students attended Jaime's class, and he openly scoffed at male dancers as being gay, probably why they stayed away. I felt deprived of male partners for Ginger Rogers/Fred Astaire style dances.

At the end of my first week, I dragged my tired body home to shower and catch a short nap. I awoke to see a limousine parked outside my window. *Just this one last time*, I decided as I dressed and primped. I insisted on sitting in the back seat, and my ride to The Daisy in plush comfort felt refreshing. I was ready for six hours of smiling and popping champagne corks.

Encouraged, almost forced, to ride in the front seat on the way home, I thanked *Limo Guy*, but discouraged him from following me around. It began to feel creepy. "I'm not scheduled to work this weekend, so I won't need a ride to The Daisy."

"That's not what Toots said."

Caught in my fib, I said, "I prefer to drive myself. *Barysh* feels neglected when I leave without him." That he understood, probably sleeps in his limo sometimes. Except for a glimpse of him driving past the studio or dropping passengers at The Daisy, he left me alone. I felt bad if I offended him, but I needed my independence.

Five days a week, three to four hours a day, Jaime pushed me without letting up as he had with the other girls. My body grew stronger and my muscles and joints less sore. Most important, my dance skills improved. All this without costing me money up to that point.

A trailer behind the studio served as his office, storage, and living space with a kitchenette and a bed. Once, when I walked in to shelve the day's music, he kicked the door shut and stood, arms folded.

"You've come a long way over the past few months, Mikel, probably as far as you or any of the girls can go." He stepped into my private space. "You must know by now why I offered you that scholarship."

I avoided eye contact but stood my ground. "Maybe you saw some talent that you could help me develop for a career in dancing?"

"True and you've arrived. Now you owe me something in return."

"I'll pay you back, but I can't do it all at once."

"I don't want your money. God created some bodies just for pleasure, to watch, enjoy, and for sex."

I backed away, but my exit had been blocked.

"Don't deny reality. Some women are like cocaine to men. The Japanese had a name for them, Geisha Girls."

He insulted me and an entire ancient culture.

"I developed you into a great dancer, probably my best work ever. It's time you face some hard facts about getting ahead in the entertainment industry." He gestured toward my lower anatomy. "Those long legs perform perfectly on the stage, now I want you to spread them for me."

"I need to leave. Now!"

"Here's the way out." He backed away and gestured toward the door, his expression showing not even a hint of disappointment. The encounter had been a business deal that fell through, or a test, or maybe a lesson.

"Class at the regular time tomorrow and bring cash. Your scholarship has run out."

I drove home, took a shower, and started to dress for work, when I heard *Limo Guy's* dreaded heavy knock on my door. I slotted the safety chain and stood off to the side as if he could see through plywood. "I won't need a ride tonight." I hadn't for the past couple of months, and I thought he got the message.

"I just dropped my passenger near here and have to head back to Hollywood. I thought, why not give my friend a ride."

A passenger from Van Nuys? Not the country club sort of people lived there.

"I just stepped out of the shower and won't be ready for a while. You better get to where you're needed." Standing naked on the other side of a paper-thin door! What fantasy did I just trigger for him?

"I'll be in my vehicle, double parked out front." His voice fading as he walked away.

What to do? After what happened at the studio, I needed reassurance that not all men were like Jaime. I dallied but not so long that I couldn't get to work on time if he drove off.

"Thanks for waiting." I accepted the passenger seat, that door held open. If Henry had seen me, his light would be on when I returned around three AM.

"It's what I do."

By the time I served the second table, thoughts of life outside The Daisy evaporated. By my fourth or fifth order, the last one requesting a bottle of champagne, lightening struck. The man was not a celebrity that I recognized, just a suave debonair hunk of masculine flesh who walked straight to a table in my section in a cloud of an exotic aroma.

"Put one of those on ice and get ready to pop the cork when my party gets here." Not only looked and smelled good, he sounded eastern European like *Limo Guy*. His party came and left after three bottles of champagne and a lot of toasting, and when I went to clear the table, his aroma lingered. I had been drawn to it like catnip, if I were a cat. I'm not sure I wasn't, the way my body purred.

Out of nowhere, he blocked my way back to the bar with a tray of dirty glasses and the empty ice bucket. He poked a finger into my shirt pocket and slid in some folded bills. "These are yours. I took care of Toots at the bar." I tingled as he tapped my breast with the back of his hand. "I'll be back."

During the limo ride home, I broke an uncomfortable silence. "Jaime propositioned me this afternoon." I decided not to mention Steve; I had caught his name as most of the toasts at the table were directed to him.

"What did Jaime say?" More interest expressed in his voice than I expected.

"That he wanted to spread my long legs." Suddenly I felt strange vibes, but what has been spoken can never be unspoken, my father's philosophy. "I'm not sure I want to go back to the studio, but I could use more fine tuning on my routines." I noticed unfamiliar street signs between The Daisy and my apartment. "Where are we going?"

"Out to Lowell Canyon. I want to show you something."

I felt uneasy. Had I not considered him a friend, I would have totally freaked. Yet, I decided to get out of the vehicle. I focused on the up-coming intersection, an all-night drug store—people. *Please green light, turn red.* The signal turned yellow and the limo bolted then braked, as a police car came into view from the side street.

One, two... a *click* before I counted *three.* Locked in!

Mom's voice: *Keep calm. Situation a big mistake. You can turn it around.*

The oversized limousine crept down and around the canyon's switchbacks, loose gravel hitting the undercarriage. He stopped at

47

a house with a single light bulb dangling inside a screened porch. Surrounded by weeds and darkness, I had no way to escape.

Mom, our plan has to work.

With a firm hold on my arm—not so tight as to bruise—he led me through the porch and up to the front door. When he fumbled with the key, I fought the urge to bolt into the darkness. The door swung open and the bulb behind us swayed. He paused to gaze at me, shadows rippling across his heavy arching brows. I felt about to be kissed, but I did not want to break eye contact, my only hope of reaching the small spot of kindness somewhere within.

I said, "Thanks for listening to my problems tonight. You are the friend I can truly trust." I made as if our immediate situation was completely ordinary. "I'm really tired and would like you to take me home now." Curved creases alongside his mouth gave him an ape-like appearance.

"I listened to what happened between you and Jaime, and I want to tell you about me."

What happened to him? He flipped the light switch and a lived-in kitchen materialized. He led me to the couch opposite the table, gestured for me to sit, but continued looming over me. "I'm Hungarian, but you probably knew that. There was part of a student protest against the Soviet Union. It turned into a full revolt, people killed on both sides."

He plopped onto the couch alongside me.

"I was too young at the time, but later I got into a situation where I shot a Russian soldier." He raised his hands in a defensive palms-out gesture. "It was him or me. I became a fugitive like thousands of other Hungarians. I got lucky, accepted as a refugee in the United States."

He paused, and I sensed a moment of indecision, maybe even tenderness. I stuck to my plan; remind him how much he really cared for me, maybe even loved me like a sister.

His eyes bulged. "I need you. I got to have you. Now!"

He lunged, tearing open my tuxedo shirt, popping the buttons. *I can sew them back on.* A strange reaction under the circumstances, but I believed I could deny his assault happened if it ended there. With my arms caught in my shirtsleeves behind my back, he ripped loose my bra. No way could I fix that!

"You don't want me this way. I know you care about me, maybe even want to make love, but not this way." He loosened his pants and exposed himself. "Please save that for when the mood is right and we can both feel okay about it."

I froze counting the seconds between flash of lightening and clap of thunder, the roar of blood pounding my eardrums and blast of hot breath washing across my face.

He rolled off me onto the floor and covered his face. A raspy whisper, "You dumb son of a bitch."

I dressed as best I could, a bundle of fear, anger, and relief. "Please take me home." It proved to be a very quiet ride until we arrived back at my apartment.

Before unlocking the door, he said, "I know you won't ever want to see me again."

"At least for now." *Forever,* I decided, but he had been kind and helpful, and he misread my reaction to our friendship. I didn't wish for a Soviet agent to abduct him and send him back to Hungary to face a firing squad, but I vowed never to talk to him again.

Boy, after that, I grew up real fast and became street smart, or so I thought. I never told my family about the incident or about a later more serious sexual attack. I didn't want their pity. Mom is beyond worrying, and the rest of my family will have to judge for themselves.

CHAPTER 7

I tossed and turned all night, my arms wrapped around the pillow end of my futon as if it had tried to escape. Two disappointing friendships and a headlong plunge into a disastrous third, if the nightmare that awakened me ever came true. I sat on the floor with my legs folded under me, repeating his name from The Daisy. *Steve, Steve*, like a star-struck teenager.

A muffled and distant ringing of Salvation Army bells set up outside The Daisy front door until Jack Hanson, the flamboyant owner, drove them across the street. His guests needed to be free of all worldly cares while tasting the fruits of their labors, or their inheritances or their sugar daddies. Am I just a tasty fruit to Steve Kostov, his name, his picture with me beside him splashed in the morning paper dropped at my doorstep?

Ice bucket in hand, I had stepped out of the photographer's range until Steve pulled me back in. "Get one of," he glanced at my name tag, "Mikel popping her cork for me." Everyone laughed, all caught in celluloid and reproduced for the local gossip rag, soggy from the morning dew.

Why did the bells keep ringing? A warning about my salvation? My phone! I released the pillow and ran to answer it.

My best friend and fellow varsity cheerleader, Teri, called to say she was coming to Los Angeles over the holidays and would like to meet up with me. Her call had meant to happen at that exact moment to save me from an improper fantasy. If she'd turned twenty one—a year behind me in school but hopefully no more than six months younger than me—Tyler and Camila could bring her to The Daisy to watch me flirt with prince charming. Had she come earlier, I might have been able to get her a walk-on part in the John Travolta movie like my friend, Doug Nelson, and I had done. She would have stories to take back home about Doug's famous movie star father, Gene Nelson. Maybe even go with me to Steve's New Year's Eve party.

Almost noon, I showered, dressed and drove to Tyler and Camila's bungalow, newspaper's entertainment section in hand; the secret in my heart, not sure Steve seriously meant to invite me to his party at his house. I had three weekends for him to show up at The Daisy and confirm the invitation.

Over the past nine months, I served celebrities but mostly married men on the make, fools I could read like a book. When Steve walked into the room decked out in black leather pants and black silk shirt opened half way to his navel and a chunk of gold dangling under his chin, I lost it. Must have been what Mom felt when Dad first entered her life.

Steve's Bulgarian roots offered more intrigue than the French, Germans, or Italians with pseudo accents to which I faked fascination for bigger tips. However, Steve emitted that new car aroma, moved through the crowd of admirers with a jaunty style. Although I was his server, never his date, he hovered around me. When seated in a different section before I began my shift, he would move his party to my area. I thought about Camila's friend, Nichole, and her lavish gift from O.J. Simpson.

I finagled a chance for my sister who was visiting over Christmas holidays with Mom to fill in for one of the girls, calling her at Tyler and Camila's house. "You have to come to The Daisy and help me out. I'm getting swamped and the rush hasn't even started."

Caroline said, "I wouldn't have the foggiest idea how to open a champagne bottle."

"It's easy. I had to learn, and you can too. I'll show you. Have Tyler take you to my place to get a tuxedo shirt and bowtie. Any black slacks will do."

"Your shirt? The sleeves won't cover my wrists."

"You can roll them up. No one will care. Just get down here, please." I glanced toward Steve's usual table still vacant. "Maybe you can meet the guy I was telling you about."

She showed and did a good job, but Steve and his entourage did not. The next night Tyler, Caroline, and Mom sat across the room from his table, but I couldn't find an opportune moment to introduce them. They claimed to be skeptical of any level of relationship with him, yet I sensed their approval, even excitement.

With Teri scheduled to arrive, I wanted to blow her socks off by taking her to Steve's party. He hadn't mentioned it again, so I used her as an excuse to remind him. "I have a friend coming to town. Would it be alright if I brought her with me to your party?"

"The more the merrier, Mikel." And I wasn't even wearing my nametag.

I'm embarrassed to admit my need to show off, but back then, I'd barely turned twenty-one, survived dance lessons at top-notch studios, and had a bit part in a John Travolta movie.

Steve claimed to have killed a man back in Bulgaria and couldn't return, overheard at his table, head-to-head in conversation with a couple of gigolos—probable drug dealers. I could spot them a mile away. I closed my eyes to his situation, the adventure, mystique, and naughtiness of it blinded me.

Teri and I arrived at the same time and circled the block before finding parking spaces. No one greeted us at the door left wide open, so we walked in and went up four or five steps to a living room with people mingling, some seated on a leather sofa and chairs. On a table, its centerpiece under a crystal chandelier, sat a bowl of cocaine as if soup to be ladled. A guy I recognized from The Daisy straightened and wiped a spot of powder from under his nose with his little finger. Like a bullfrog, he flicked his tongue and the white disappeared.

"Hi, Mikel. Steve's upstairs." He and Teri exchanged names and headed toward a group hanging around the kitchen.

Up a second half-flight of stairs, a man with a smile I shouldn't have trusted pointed to a closed door.

"Go on in."

I opened to see Steve's exposed butt, his hands groping a naked female who squealed in an accent different from his, mine exploding in good old Albuquerque English, "You Bastard!"

Let me explain, the usual favorite line from any movie, but not from Steve. His, so *what?* expression for his behavior, natural, normal, and appropriate. Before the last syllable of *bastard* spilled into the hallway, I ran out the door and to the kitchen.

I found Teri, but at a loss for the appropriate words, I simply asked, "Are you enjoying the party?"

"This is fun."

I could see it, surrounded by suitors offering drinks and laughing at lame jokes. I decided to stay for her sake. When I noticed *naked girl*, now dressed, flush, and freshly sexed, I charged upstairs to give Steve a piece of my mind.

Shirtless, he grabbed me and threw me on the bed.

"Now I'm ready for you," as if he needed a warm-up session before taking me on.

Not since the day at South Padre Island with Stephen, or the trailer with Jaime, or at that abandoned house with *Limo Guy* had I felt such panic. This time I bolted. Steve blocked my exit, so I ran to the window. Locked! One quick glance back and Kostov's leer clearly stated his intention. *You're mine now, baby.* I raised my knee—if only he had been standing in front of me—and reached back to slip off one of my spiked heels. One whack and spider webs raced across the glass, my second swing interrupted by his arms wrapping around my midsection. He dragged me to the bed, flung me back first onto rumpled sheets, and pounced on top of me. I probably landed a punch and made a couple of face scratches before he pinned my arms above my head.

"You little Bitch!" He called to the *other woman* who appeared in the doorway, purse strap slung over her shoulder. "Give me one."

She retrieved a small bottle, shaking a pill loose and approaching me, pill pinched between finger and thumb, gestured for me to open my mouth. Steve released one hand from restraining my wrists and punched me in the eye, his thumb prying my mouth open and *Lady-Friend* jamming the pill inside. I was overpowered and my last conscious thought, a prayer, an act of contrition. I thought I would be killed.

I woke up naked with Steve naked along side me. Too scared to scream, I slipped from the bed, located my clothes, and locked myself in the bathroom. Facing mirrors I wished weren't there, I dressed, tiptoed out of the room, and down the stairs. Other than a few snoring bodies the place was empty, Teri nowhere to be found. She probably figured I decided to sleep over. *Barysh*, sitting lonely down the street, wheeled me like a gurney to my apartment where I hid for a week.

Then came a knocking at my door.

 CHAPTER 8

I stood under the shower until the hot water turned cold, until my knees buckled and I dropped to the floor too numb to shiver, yet not washed clean. The old man whose friendliness ran hot and cold like the water in our side-by-side apartments banged on the common bathroom wall between us. I twisted the knob and the spray stopped. I hesitated to face the mirrors. My left eye felt like it had been replaced with a baseball, and I couldn't lift my eyelid. Opening my mouth made me wince, but I refused to cry out. I counted my teeth with my tongue and found no gaps.

The tiger in me gave up. I crawled to my futon and curled back into the womb. Nine months and I could be a new person, the old one too damaged to salvage.

About the second day of my isolation, I shivered with fear. Rumor had it that Kostov killed a man in Bulgaria. *Limo Guy* killed a soldier back in Hungary. One or the other is coming to keep me quiet. I won't tell anyone, I promise. I would never admit to such disgrace, my shame. A *grrr* rose from deep within my throat. My tiger stirred.

Two more days of soda crackers and water, I felt faint but not hunger. Reluctantly, I opened a can of soup. Another day to take that first sip. And to sort out my future.

My scholarship had been canceled, but I still had a job at The Daisy. Or, did I? I can't take my next shift for two reasons, my black-and-blue face and their customer who caused it, Kostov.

My tiger reacted. *I have never quit anything in my life.* And it receded. *I wouldn't be quitting, only moving on.* I called Toots and gave my notice. She told me to forget my shift and to pick up my final check next week. Had my assailants turned her against me? Would both men be bragging about what they had done?

Teri! I thanked the stars—not ready to invoke God just yet—that she disappeared and hadn't seen me like this. Last I saw of her, she was having the time of her life. What must she think of me now?

My tiger roared. I no longer feared being killed but wanted to kill, or at least wished Kostov dead. Maybe he and *Limo Guy* will kill each other, seems to be their pattern. I checked the mirror, bruises noticeable but passable with makeup. Will I ever trust a man again? The damage done to my body will repair itself soon, my devastated spirit, probably longer. Maybe never.

Then came Doug Nelson knocking at my door.

"Mikel, are you in there?"

Go away!

"I see your car out front. Open the door."

One, one-thousand; two, one-thousand; three, one-thousand.... I stopped counting at ten, and still no sound. Had he given up?

"I going to call Dad and he'll send the police."

No such luck. "What do you want?"

"To know that you're okay."

"I'm alright. Now go away."

"Next week they're starting auditions at Universal Studio for a Michael J. Fox movie. Dad said to get in line before the word gets around."

A force in me awakened strong enough to budge the heavy weight of the past week. Only a small walk-on part in the Travolta movie, but I had a taste of acting. "If I let you in, will you promise to keep a secret?"

"Sure, what is it?"

"Do you promise?"

"I said I would."

"I'll unlock the door. Count to ten before you open it."

"Are you sure you're okay?"

"Just do as I tell you."

"One, two, three..."

I clicked the lock open and retreated to my futon, arm hugging my knees, my body rocking slightly.

"Ten. Ready or not, here I come."

I was not in the mood for his cute little game of hide-and-seek, or for the splash of sunlight when the door swung open. I shielded my eyes and felt my robe gape open. We were friends, maybe kissed but never into any heavy petting. I pulled my robe tight around me, but my breasts had been uncovered.

"Wow! What happened to your face?"

"I was raped." I blurted what I had promised myself never to utter. In one careless second, Doug learned my secret. *Once admitted, the truth can never be retracted.*

"Holy shit. We gotta report this to the police. Get dressed, or don't bother. I'm getting my car from down the street."

"I'm not going," still stuck in my throat, I exchanged my robe for a shirt, stepped into a pair of slacks, and carried my sneakers to his car. In those few seconds, our relationship took a giant leap forward, and it frightened me.

A detective at Santa Monica Police Department snapped pictures of my face, not the part of my body that still mattered, and took my statement. I told her I didn't know who raped me because it was dark.

"You were at a party, not some back alley. Give us a list of guests. We'll sort it out for you."

I actually believed she could legally toss darts at fifty names and find one bad guy. "He will kill me."

"We'll protect you."

I sobbed, "Steve Kostov."

The detective cracked the first smile of her interview.

"Are you going to arrest him?"

She tucked her camera into its case. "We'll question him, but we already know what he'll say."

I cringed. "That I agreed to have sex with him?"

"He is a persuasive guy."

"What about this?" I touched my eyelid and felt a normal sized eyeball. "I'm still black and blue."

"Some of the women he hangs around with like it a little rough." She aimed the pen at me like a gun. "Listen. You were at his party. Probably had some drinks, maybe even snorted a little powder." She shoved the report across the table.

"I didn't...." I glanced at it barely recognizing my handwriting.

"Is there anything else you would like to add?"

He drugged me stuck to in my throat and burned like hot pepper. Who would believe I hadn't been doing drugs? I didn't run from the house when I saw the cocaine setting in the open. My hand shook as I picked up the pen and signed the report.

"We'll keep your complaint on file, and you'll hear from us if we learn anything."

"Is that all?"

"You can bring us the results of a rape-kit from the hospital. Might be a good idea to have it on file."

The test confirmed that I recently had sex, probably not as a virgin, and that I had been beaten. However, after a lapse of a week, the obvious connection would not hold up in court. *Thanks a lot for exposing my private life to my new boyfriend, if either one of us still wanted to continue any sort of relationship.*

Doug remained silent the entire ride back to my apartment, and my embarrassment overrode my fear and anger. *What must he think of me?*

Pulling up to my apartment, he answered my unasked question. "I'm glad you weren't a virgin, or the ordeal would have been harder to get over."

Just Stephen back in high school. I caught myself before exposing our secret since the senior prom.

At my door, he said, "I won't tell anyone what happened, and we don't ever have to talk about it again."

I could learn to love that guy.

"I'll pick you up tomorrow morning, and we can stand in line at Universal Studios like we did for the Travolta movie."

I pointed to my eye, now wide open but still throbbing.

"You'll look good in Hollywood sunglasses. I'll get you a pair on my way over here. Seven o'clock sharp."

I opened the door and stepped into what had been a cozy retreat at the end of a hard day now reeking of bad memories. I turned and mumbled, "Thanks. You're a good friend." My gaze wandered between the half-consumed bowl of soup and my robe balled up on my futon. "I'll be ready."

I undressed, ditched another outfit into the wastebasket, and turned the shower on full blast. Henry won't have hot water for the next few hours. Emerging from the bathroom dripping wet and feeling clean, I retrieved my crumpled robe.

I remained optimistic, yet alert to danger, vulnerable but cautious. My new rule of thumb: if you wake up with a hickey and a black eye, it is time to reevaluate the relationship.

Hot soup with crackers tasted quite good.

I collapsed onto my futon in turmoil of emotions. My assailant will get off, but I won't ever have to face him again.

I had met Doug a few months earlier during the filming of *Perfect* with John Travolta, Jamie Lee Curtis, and Marilu Henner. The production crew went on location to a flower shop in Van Nuys for a two-minute scene. Douglas M. Nelson and Mikel J. Peterson were staged as a couple buying flowers when John Travolta entered. We walked off the set with our purchase, were relieved of the bouquet, and excused from the scene. We strolled hand-in-hand down the street to a motor-sport store where I spotted the same jacket Travolta wore in the flower shop scene.

"I gotta have that." Doug grabbed my hand and pulled me into the store.

Although we never actually met before the flower-shop scene, I knew Douglas Nelson was from a movie star family, his father, Gene Nelson, a famous dancer/actor. I assumed he could afford an expensive leather jacket and that he might be spoiled enough to feel a need to own it. I was glad that he never wore it on the set throughout the rest of the filming.

***

Happy New Year, 1984! Three hundred and sixty six days—thank God for leap year. I didn't know it then, but I needed that extra time to fit in the Summer Olympics and wedding plans. I drifted off, relieved that Mom remained unaware her daughter had been raped. I fell asleep with pleasant memories nudging out the bad ones.

The morning after my humiliation with the detective, Doug knocked on my door at seven o'clock. By ten, a couple dozen of us had clustered outside Universal Studio hoping for a part in the Michael J. Fox movie.

A guy shouted, "You there!" He aimed his megaphone at us. "Are you two a couple?"

Doug grabbed my arm and pulled me through the crowd. "Yeah, we're together. This is my girlfriend, Mikel," like he was an established actor introducing a neophyte. Granted, he had been in a couple of movies as a child, but Gene Nelson never pulled any strings to boost his son's acting career like other famous fathers. I doubt Doug ever forgave his dad.

"Do you play basketball?"

"Yup, varsity."

"And you, can you dance?"

"I trained at Debby Reynold's Studio." No way I could have uttered Jaime Roger's name and continue smiling.

"Take off the glasses."

He studied my face, and then flashed an accusing glance at Doug.

"She just had some minor plastic surgery."

Douglas Nelson, you rat.

"Go on in. Next!"

Our parts in the movie, *Teen Wolf,* took place at a local high school. Doug appeared in the basketball sequences and a few classroom settings. My scenes included students gathering in the hallway between classes and the school dance in the gym. The director liked my enthusiasm and facial expressions, keeping me in view of the camera. I followed his direction explicitly, careful never to upstage the main actors.

Sometimes, an extra actor will add a little gesture to brag about hoping it wouldn't be cut, not always befitting the scene. If caught, the director would kick him or her off the set. One such antic occurred in the last kissing scene between Michael and his costar. A guy seated alone in the bleachers stood as if to leave and flashed his opened fly. Even today on the internet, movie buffs claim they can see a bit of a penis. I checked it out and guess what—he was the same redheaded fellow who pissed off Doug by flirting with me. If I could recall his name, it would be fun to expose the rest of him as a spoilsport.

Once during break from the set, we went strolling through local shops where I found a stuffed toy moose. "Let's buy it and give it to Michael. He's from Alberta, Canada, and would appreciate a little reminder from home."

We delivered it to the back-lot trailer with *Michael J. Fox* above the door, and he invited us in for sodas. He was Doug's age, two years older than me, and he loved the moose. Throughout the rest of the filming, he remembered our names and told us that he and his moose were getting along just fine.

The movie turned out to be a dud. Michael redeemed himself with *Back to the Future*, a movie for which I didn't try out. A better opportunity came my way. My Gemini kept plugging for me.

CHAPTER 9

When the filming stopped, and editors performed their surgery to trim a few hours off camera time to a ninety-one-minute movie, and the marketing people declared its official title, *Teen Wolf*, the buzz around the studio turned to auditions for dancers in the '84 Summer Olympics' opening ceremony.

Barysh got a little hot under his hood, as I pushed him along the steep grades of Laurel Canyon Boulevard toward Los Angeles. When I reached Third Street, I panicked. The line-up of hopeful dancers on the sidewalk outside the building seemed to go on forever. I drove on by.

Glancing into the rear view mirror, I whispered through gritted teeth, "You came all this way, and you are going to audition like everyone else."

Joining the block-long line of mostly females trying out that morning, I nearly wished I had been born male. However, I decreased each of those girls' chances by one. Sorry, but I am here to win.

I returned to my car after the Los Angeles hills had eaten half the April sun, and the sharp, long shadows stretched across the boulevard began to dissolve. *Cathedral time*, my mother claimed, and I whispered a prayer of thanks. The effect of my achievement slowly swelled to a crescendo on my way home. Seeing Doug parked in front of my apartment, I burst into tears, not sure if I felt joy or pain.

Doug ran to the curb, jerked open the passenger door, and cast his eyes down. "You didn't get the part?"

I broke into a hysterical laughing fit.

"Are you all right?"

I grabbed the lapels of his jacket and yanked him nearly onto my lap, the steering wheel not withstanding.

"Ouch! What was that all about?"

"I got it. I'm going to be in the Olympics." I released one lapel and pinched his cheeks until his lips puckered. "On television, all over the world."

"You gonna to kish me?"

I patted his puckered lips back into shape. *I am going to make love to you.* What had I just about promised him? "Not today."

"Well, if you aren't going to kiss me today, let's go inside and you can tell me everything that happened."

"You read my mind." Thankfully, he did not. "Come on. We'll celebrate with a glass of lemonade."

"Better yet. If you let go of my jacket, I'll get the champagne from my car."

I grabbed *Barysh* by his steering wheel and held tight. "No need. I'm already dizzy with happiness."

On the walk to my apartment, I pulled the key from my purse, Doug already at my door waving bottle and corkscrew. "Don't announce it to the whole neighborhood."

He yelled, "My girlfriend is going to be in the Olympics, and we're celebrating."

Girlfriend? Maybe tonight. Gemini, back off! "Quiet or we'll have Henry to contend with."

We sat across from each other at the kitchen table sipping and toasting. "The dance numbers were easy, no jumping knee slides. Some Ginger Rogers and Fred Astaire ballroom routines." A sudden embarrassment over my gloating. "How about your day? What did you get?"

"Just the usual comedy clubs. I developed another celebrity voice, up to twenty now."

"No movies?"

"If only Dad would show a little interest in my acting career, but he's into directing TV soap operas these days." He scanned the living area of my studio apartment, eyes settling on its centerpiece, my burgundy self-styled futon.

Distracted from a vacant stare, Doug's gaze shot directly at me. "Let's you and me get an apartment in a nicer area."

"Ha. I couldn't even afford this one, if it weren't for Mom and our friend Jim kicking in with rent money."

"I got some cash." He glanced up at the ceiling as if it were stashed up there. "My insurance settlement. And I'm bound to get acting jobs, if I keep pounding the pavement." His gaze returned. "You will get paid, won't you?"

"Not much more than our movie roles. I signed a contract that starts next week and runs through the opening ceremony at the end of July."

"Let's get something to eat." Thankfully, he abandoned the idea of us moving in together, probably caught my hesitation. I wouldn't mind returning home nights and cozying up to him, not since Stephen back in Albuquerque had I been so tempted. Maybe Kostov before... I shuddered and blocked an ugly memory. "I'm more tired than hungry."

"In other words, you want me to leave," his expression hopeful or compliant, I couldn't tell.

Yes, but his hangdog expression broke my heart. "Tell you what. You get some Chinese take-out while I shower. After we eat, you can hit the road and I'll hit the hay."

I fell asleep in my futon, his arms wrapped around me, and we had cold chow mein for breakfast.

Seven days without dance lessons, waitressing, or acting, I loved and disliked the feeling of freedom. Except for Sunday—I dragged Doug along to church—my routine felt out of kilter.

However, cruising Los Angeles' freeways in Doug's convertible with the top down, I imagined Mom's life before Jim, even before Dad captured her heart. She must have felt on top of the world. Between having babies with Dr. Peterson, she devoured every adventure Albuquerque had to offer gallivanting around in Marylyn Monroe's Cadillac.

From Disney Land in Anaheim to the shops of Venice Beach, between the grungy LaBrae tar pits and the theme park at Universal Studios, we explored everything Los Angeles had to offer us and every thrill we could offer each other. We strolled along the fifteen-block Hollywood Walk of Fame rooting for our favorite stars.

"Where is your dad's hand print?" I asked seven years prematurely.

"He hasn't been recognized yet, but I'm sure it will happen."

Had I not been saved by a full-time dance contract from the Olympic committee, I would have been swept off course by the delights of exploring our new relationship. My small apartment, almost womb-like, remained my refuge five nights a week, opened to allow Doug access on weekends. He complained graciously but allowed me freedom to pursue my dream of a dancing career.

I called my sister Caroline to toot my horn, and she shared her good news. She graduated *magna cum laude* from Abilene Christian College—I was not surprised—and she secured an interview for a scholarship in the osteopathic program at California State Polytechnic University at Pomona.

"I'll pick her up at the airport." Doug to the rescue. "How will I recognize her?"

"Keep a lookout for a female head sticking out above the crowd who doesn't look like me."

"With that description, I might bring back any number of women."

"Just one, and don't worry, Caroline will admit that she's my sister."

We had very little time together, she sweating acceptance into their osteopathic program, and me preparing for the Olympic opening ceremony. The three of us dined out, Doug selecting the restaurant and generously picking up the tab.

After his toasting Caroline and me for our successes, I asked a favor. "Will you bring me to rehearsal tomorrow, so Caroline can drive *Barysh* to Pomona?"

"I'll take your sister to her interview and wait for her."

Caroline readily accepted his better offer. "I'll be a nervous wreck as it is without having to face California freeways."

"My pleasure. Who knows, maybe someday you'll become my sister." Doug's most coy voice.

Caroline's eyes rolled in my direction. "I see."

I attempted to change the subject. "Doesn't Doug have good taste in restaurants?"

Caroline raised her nearly empty glass. "Here's to the man who may have stolen my sister's heart."

That night my futon experienced an entirely different kind of workout, bodies back to back, arms and legs splayed in all directions. We awoke to Doug's knocking at the door.

"Donuts and coffee if you let me in."

We scrambled to look presentable, and made Doug wait a respectable amount of time.

Our second evening together, a repeat with the three of us dining, Caroline's mood changed from anxious to one of satisfaction. After the interview that afternoon, a young intern who sat in on the meeting followed her into the restroom. She told Caroline that everyone in the committee really liked her responses.

"Does that mean you're accepted into the program?" Doug asked.

"I felt good vibes from the lead doctor. And I have a new friend." My sister flashed a glance my way. "We exchanged phone numbers."

Caroline and I sat up talking until early hours in the morning, sharing who we were and what we wanted for our futures. Both of our lives took dramatic turns that night. In my case, Doug will get the kind of commitment he wants from me, and Caroline decided to come out of the closet, practicing with telling Doug. He nonchalantly nodded his understanding, but his cheeks reddened. I was proud of him, again.

The day after Caroline left, I gave my landlord a thirty-day notice, and Doug and I began looking at apartments in Beverly Hills, his choice of city, not necessarily mine. I had been preoccupied with rehearsals for the opening ceremonies. Doug didn't seem to mind making all the decisions, even purchasing additional furniture above what he already had. He would show pictures from brochures, and I always suggested something less expensive. Only when I thought the two-bedroom apartment he suggested might be too expensive did he readily agree.

His usual response: "I have it covered."

He and a friend with a pickup moved his belongings into our new apartment. The purchased items were delivered. *Barysh* brought all my stuff in a single trip. All but the futon. The young Hispanic girl who came to view my studio apartment eyed my creation.

"You make that yourself?"

I nodded.

"Will you help me make one like it?"

"It's yours. I won't need it anymore." I imitated Doug's generosity, and it felt good. He had already slept on our new bed two nights, waiting for the weekend when I would move in.

"How does it feel to have sex in our very own bed?" Doug asked, laying back and staring at the ceiling.

"Wonderful?" I missed my futon. And possibly my freedom.

CHAPTER 10

Every time I watch a video of the '84 summer Olympics' opening ceremony, I experience much of what I felt that day. The extravaganza anticipated through piecemeal segments performed during practice rehearsals cannot compare to David L. Wolper's three-and-a-half-hour, non-stop event in full costume with the roar of ninety-thousand people in the bleachers.

Admittedly, I couldn't see any parts while waiting in the sidelines for our segment to begin, and not much more than those dancers close to me while performing on the field and up on the stage, but my in-person sensation remained breathtaking. Scanning the crowd, I located President Ronald Regan and Nancy.

The video captured the overall ceremony, but only having been there can recreate the thrilling sensations. With *Eighty-Four* as the Olympic theme, that many positions were divided between male and female dancers, a few allotted to very talented children. Of the fifteen thousand costumes in the performance, my group of dances made three changes. I still have one of mine created for the Ginger Rogers/Fred Astaire number. David L. Wolper signed on Ron Field (not to be confused with Kenneth Feld of *Siegfried and Roy*) who earned a Tony Award for *Cabaret* in 1966 to choreograph our dance segments.

My partner—obviously gay according to Douglas—and I practiced diligently to make up for my inexperience with opposite-sex dance partners. Deprived of male dancers in Jaime's class, I had not been paired with a fellow since back at Joe Tremaine's Studio.

Rocket Man opened the ceremony by zooming onto the field in a jet suit awakening one hundred and twenty trumpets and twenty timpani drums. Next, the fifteen minute overture, "Olympic Fanfare and Theme" with the hundred-piece Olympic Symphony Orchestra conducted by composer John Williams, famous as musical director in the movies *Jaws* and *Star Wars*.

A twelve-hundred person marching band released as many balloons and began their synchronized formations back and forth across the field, ending in an outline of the United States of America. Musical choices represented American genre: jazz, gospel, swing, folk, Dixieland, Broadway shows, and the big band era.

Our first choreographed number represented the American pioneer westward movement, but due to the dominant Roman-arched stage above the bleachers to the east, we entered from the west side of the human outlined map. Decked out in frontier Americana, men wore buckskins, the women full-skirted dresses and bonnets, and the children dressed in simple frocks and britches with suspenders. Women and children danced to the center of the arena followed by nine replicated but human-propelled covered wagons; oxen would have been unmanageable with ninety-thousand people cheering them on. Like Greek warriors hiding in the Trojan horse, five male dancers sprang from each unit, but, unlike the warriors, these dancers broke apart their wagons, wheels still rotating. A touch of real history, they used the cargo and the disassembled wagon parts to erect buildings: a house with a white picket fence, a bakery, a general store, a bank, a hotel, a saloon, and a school, Hollywood's techniques of creating fake scenery.

When the school bell rang, the flag was raised, and the music and dance turned country hoedown with "Buffalo Gals, Won't You Come Out Tonight?" The crowd went mad, and I got goose bumps on top of goose bumps.

Our second dance performance followed the marching band's series of formations that ended in an outline of a riverboat with a rotating paddle wheel. Dressed in turn-of-the-century southern costumes, we jumped and tumbled and did modified knee slides to Dixieland Jazz.

Our third and final number was the most spectacular. Behind the main dance platform erected above the east-side bleachers, fourteen colonnaded alcoves staged six grand pianos—eighty-four total—in pairs facing one another. A thousand-member choir flanked by a five-hundred-piece orchestra with ninety-six trombones and one hundred and forty-four trumpets, spread over the bleachers below the stage, all conducted by John Williams.

Women wore white and silver bodices with turquoise flowing overlays, the men in white pants with ruffled shirts, dancing in pairs to a medley of George Gershwin songs. We worked our way up the bleachers, and when in place across the stage, the orchestra, accompanied by eighty-four pianos, began Gershwin's "Rhapsody in Blue." The effect was beyond incredible and it still gives me those double goose bumps.

One of the decisions that would not stand today was the criteria for selecting eighty-four pianists. They had to have keyboard skills and penises. Since Gershwin presumably had one, Wolper recruited only male piano players. If he had applied that rule to our *Frontier Americana* number, the set would have only needed a general store and a saloon.

Raves across the media claimed the finale piece to be the Olympic highlight, second only to eight thousand athletes from one-hundred-and-forty countries marching onto the field in the

Parade of Nations. As the participating athletes entered, the band played that nation's anthem and sections from the bleachers held up pre-arranged colored placards to display their living flag.

We performers lined up as the athletes passed and exchanged small pins handed out earlier. I still have the ones I managed to trade. I waved as Mary Lou Retton, America's gold medal gymnast, marched past me, and a private joke popped into my head. *You're just lucky my legs grew too long.*

My family watched Jim McKay of ABC Sports and Peter Jennings of World News Tonight emcee the three-and-a-half hour opening ceremony. People living in Greater Los Angeles heard the bells from every church in the area ring out when the balloons were released. I doubt any of my friends were able to acquire a two hundred dollar ticket.

 CHAPTER 11

After the opening ceremonies, I changed into street clothes and gathered my belongings, including my third and last costume. Between acts, dancers tossed their costumes onto a pile in a haste to make their changes, no one cataloging or even treating them with care.

The lady gathering them asked, "Would you like to keep yours? They're only going to be discarded anyway."

A grin spread across my face, and I tucked the white and silver bodice with turquoise flowing overlay into my bag and headed toward the exit where Doug agreed to meet me.

Some invisible obstacle just outside the door split the thinning crowd into two diverging sections, and as I walked, I heard laughing and cheering. The couple ahead of me paused as if unsure which direction to deflect. They split apart and Doug appeared, on knee, eyes fixed ahead, arm extended. Nestled in his palm sat an opened white box, set on a mound of silk, a diamond ring.

"Michelle Peterson, will you marry me?"

My first thought, *put that thing away before someone grabs it and runs off.* Second thought, *no, I won't.* Third, *maybe.* I grasped his hand, box, and all. "Yes, Douglas Nelson, I will."

The remnants of the crowd cheered. A male voice, "Hey, she's one of the dancers."

Bursting with pride, I shouted back, "Yes, I am." I shot my arms into the air and did a hooray jump. "And I am going to marry this guy." Glancing down, I noticed part of my costume had peeked out of my garment bag. The man recognized me, not my costume, I assured myself.

Doug continued to extend the box. "Here, try it on."

We strutted off to Doug's car, engaged.

He said, "My parents invited us to dinner tonight. They both want to meet you, especially Dad after watching you dance today."

"He had tickets to the opening ceremony?"

"He has connections, not that it does me any good. Probably going to some of the games, too."

I shook my head. "I don't know. I'm pretty tired."

"When we get home, you can take a quick nap."

"Where would we be eating or better yet, what should I wear?"

"Put on your cowgirl outfit from the country hoedown. That would impress him."

No cowgirl outfit and definitely not the costume that came home with me. "What about your mother?"

"Don't worry about Mother." He stretched *mother* into three syllables. "You don't own anything expensive enough to impress her."

"The nap sounds good." However, I knew it wouldn't happen. I needed every minute to get myself ready to meet these important people.

I had not met either parent, but Doug had spouted Gene Nelson's name at the studio to impress the directors and actors or even kids like us with walk-on parts. His dad had starring roles in *Carousel* and *Oklahoma* with Gordon MacRae and Shirley Jones and probably many more.

Gene arrived at the restaurant without Marilyn M. Fields offering neither excuse nor an apology. "This way I get you all to myself." He took my outstretched hand about to kiss it, I think, but I wrapped my arms around him. He reciprocated and I had found my second father.

"Show Dad the ring. Don't hide it."

Self-conscious, I had broken from my hug and returned my hand to my side, nervously thumbing the band on my finger. "Sorry." I displayed the diamond.

"That's very nice. Congratulations to both of you."

"Doug tells me that you were at the opening ceremonies today."

"Wolper called me and we discussed the Fred Astaire and Ginger Rogers' theme. I told him a very special girl will be part of that number, but I didn't mention whom. When things settle down, I'll tell him, if he hadn't already guessed."

The smug expression on Doug's face couldn't hide his enjoying my embarrassment at his father's flattery. How could I ever live up to Gene's expectations after his son's exaggeration of my talent?

The Maitre d' led us to our table. Gene seated me and took the chair alongside, across from Doug. "Did Lionel Richie talk to you?"

"How did you hear about that?" I had a hunch I'd been selected to dance during his closing number, but wasn't going to say anything until I knew for sure.

"I didn't, but watching you dance, he certainly recognized your talent. I believe he wants a dozen girls, probably all white to balance his Harlem Theater Dancers."

I had met his expectations! The rest of the evening whizzed by in dizzying fashion. I had been swept off my feet before, always aware who or what created my internal turmoil. That night, the flutter of my heart seemed to be the combination of an Olympic high, my engagement, the champagne, Gene Nelson, and his son, unfortunately, in that order.

***

Except for Sundays, rehearsals with Lionel Richie happened daily for two weeks between opening and closing ceremonies, and by the end of each session, I came home exhausted. Doug would have a tub of hot water ready; me soaking alone, but he got to rub my sore muscles and maybe draw on my last bit of energy in bed later.

Sunday, after attending church service, routine for me but a new experience for Doug, he scheduled a meeting with his mother. From earlier conversations, I had the impression that he was closer to her than to Gene, yet he dallied the afternoon of our appointment.

"Mom is different than Dad."

"How so?"

"Well, she's a bit protective of me. I'm her only son."

"I've have a mother who would give her life for her children." In a sense, she had done so when raising Caroline and me.

"After my accident with the doctors and lawyers and all, she sort of took control and hasn't entirely let go." He avoided eye contact. "She might ask embarrassing questions."

"I'm sure she will like me." Winning adult approval had been my specialty. I had friends, of course, but their parents, especially the mothers, readily accepted me.

"We'll see, but don't be surprised. You know she snubbed us the night we had dinner with Dad."

I assumed as much, but hadn't given her the benefit of even caring.

Driving along Sunset Boulevard, I marveled at the houses, and when Doug turned onto a winding road, they became more and more elaborate. He stopped at the end of the lane where an attendant opened the gate for us to drive up to an immense mansion. I was flabbergasted. Doug told me his mother had remarried, and I wondered how much of Gene's money went with her after their divorce?

"I'm getting frightened, Doug. Do you think she will like me?"

"I love you and that's all that matters."

That should have been my first clue. A woman bedecked in jewels, bouffant flawless, sashayed to greet us at the front entry. She never offered her hand or even made eye contact.

"Is this the friend you told me about, Douglas?"

"She's more than a friend, Mother. We're engaged." He grabbed my wrist and shoved the back of my hand in front of his mother's face. "See the ring."

I displayed my ring finger.

She showed no emotion. "Come, we need to talk."

I looked at Doug wondering if she meant me.

He blushed. "I'll see what she wants."

Barely out of sight, she yelled, "What do you mean by bringing that dancer into our family? She's only after your insurance money."

I went to the car and waited for Doug.

He came out shortly, slid onto the driver's seat, and pounded the steering wheel. "You must have heard that."

"So did all the neighbors." I glanced around and noticed there weren't any.

"You know, it doesn't change anything."

I nodded, placing the incident in the back of my mind, not sure if it would disappear or loom and destroy our relationship. I understood a mother trying to keep a son from making a mistake, but in this case, the mistake would have been mine. I wasn't ready to settle down to a life in Beverly Hills.

The final week of rehearsals, I did not let anything distract me from my dance routine. I had to blend with a troupe where most of the dancers had previously worked together. The choreography was new to everyone, but I needed some catch-up with break dancing from the streets of the Bronx back in the seventies. Forced back into the mindset from Jaime Rogers' hard core training, I reflected on his other aspect I had blocked. Intentional or not, his opening my eyes to the brutal realities of my career choice should have armed me against two vicious assaults. No such problem during the Olympics, but I needed Jaime's two pronged vision of what I was up against in the future. For the closing ceremony, I concentrated on his vigorous stamina contribution to my performance.

Cuba Gooding Jr., a kid four years younger than me, did a break-dance sequence with some other black street dancers, including a vertical body spin, upside-down with only the dancer's head contacting the floor.

Lionel Richie wore a glistening blue jacket over white slacks and shoes, his female partner in red. Most of us wore white with a few decked out in blue. An inner and outer circle of dancers formed the outline of a space ship, a straw-hat shape with head-band and brim outlined. A sparkling platform rose from center stage, on it Richie and his partner led us in nine minutes of nonstop action. Floor jets spewed confetti that floated onto the dancers like snowflakes.

The spaceship theme became apparent when a genuine UFO soared from outer space, intersected with the full moon, and hovered above the stadium. Its one-hundred-and-sixty-foot perimeter of flashing lights resembled our dance formation, as if a primitive tribe of humans gyrating around a bonfire had caught the attention of an advanced civilization.

On command, ninety-thousand spectators welcomed the invaders by waving blue reflective flags, and the space visitors responded with a show of light across the sea of shimmering blue.

After hovering and shooting laser beams with zapping sounds in all directions, it glided back over the abandoned stage where the eighty-four grand pianos had performed in pillared alcoves during the opening ceremony. Explosions of light filled each alcove as fireworks shot up suggesting a spectacular landing just outside the stadium. A man over seven feet tall in a space suit with an umbilical cord attached entered the central archway and waved to the crowd, officially closing the 1984 Olympics.

CHAPTER 12

"When can I meet your mother?" Doug asked, probably feeling guilty after having tea at Marilyn M. Fields' mansion without me. He hadn't invited me along, and I didn't suggest I should go.

"Mom was just here last Christmas with Caroline. I suppose she might be willing to break away from church and Jim for a few days."

"Invite her friend to come, too."

"She and Jim won't travel as a couple. Overnight together would send the wrong message."

A wave of nostalgia for snow and Christmas lights swept over me. "You and I are going to Albuquerque this Christmas."

Doug didn't seem to share my enthusiasm. I asked, "Are you afraid to meet my family?" I had told him about the madhouse of siblings, in-laws, and their off spring that descended on Mom's house over the holidays.

"I want to meet all of them. I thought meeting your parents first would be more proper."

"Like my meeting your mother?" That sounded more snotty than intended.

He stammered, "Mom…"

"I'm sorry, I didn't mean to be nasty."

"I'm trying to tell you that Mother wants to see you again."

"At her place or ours?" Hurt or anger, I wasn't sure which, still lingered from our first encounter.

"At José Eber's."

"A restaurant?" Maybe in a public place she will act more civil.

"José Eber is Mom's hair stylist."

"We're going to have our hair done together? How girl-like."

"Not together, but she will meet you there after your appointment. She'll take care of the details."

"Including the tip?" I still couldn't take her offer serious.

"Please, she just wants to do something nice for you. From there you two will go shopping and have lunch at a nice restaurant."

I was too stunned to respond.

Douglas switched topics. "Christmas in Albuquerque sounds good, but that's five months away. Let me buy your mother an airline ticket right now."

"I'll do it."

"You can't afford it."

"No, I mean I'll meet with your mother, beauty salon, shopping spree, and restaurant. The total package." His put-down about money needed a response. "I *can* afford to pay for Mom's flight to meet her future son-in-law." To avoid his dreaded apology, I added, "Save your money for next December." I salvaged some of my dignity.

Mom accepted my offer, but Jim insisted he pay. To refuse would have offended him, but we agreed to go fifty-fifty.

In the meantime, I had an appointment to have my hair done.

***

"You look beautiful. How did it go with Mother?" Douglas' comment and question blurted in the proper order, as I returned from his mother/fiancé social experiment.

I responded in reverse order. "We can tolerate each other, and thank you for the compliment. Do you like me with highlights?"

"I'd love you in any hairdo.

Thankfully, my new look distracted him from asking more questions about my afternoon with his mother. I needed time to sort out my feelings. Had Marilyn M. Fields intended to introduce me to her world of glamour or to frighten me away from her son?

"The full treatment," exclaimed José Eber, whose posture implied *professional dancer*, but definitely not at Jaime's studio. "She'll be dining with Mrs. Fields this afternoon."

A simple *wash your hands before eating* becomes a *full make over* before lunch with socialite Marilyn M. Fields.

Like an innocent lamb, I bleated, "Not blond, please."

José Eber's reaction resembled an artist denied a basic color on his palette. "Only a highlight, but full facial." He disappeared and hours later reappeared with the future mother-in-law in tow. Gushing over his completed masterpiece somewhat softened her irritation with having to wait beyond the estimated time.

Shopping at the Beverly Center went more smoothly. I contained my shock at the prices, but the quality and style would have pleased my mother. In fact, I gained some insights into my mother, Doug's mother, and myself. Betty Jeanne Peterson achieved a comfortable level of sophistication with limited funds, whereas Marilyn M. Fields, with unlimited resources, always needed to prove that she fit in high society.

Before entering the restaurant, Doug's mother inspected my new outfit for any possible wrinkle or flaw. A tiny thread caught her attention, and she acted as if soup had been spilled on the fabric. Once seated, I impressed her with my dinner etiquette instilled by my mother every time we sat down to eat. I resisted getting up to clear the table when a course was completed.

This revelation about my mother and Doug's mother created an *aha* moment for me. I realized where I belonged on the continuum between the two women. The experience transformed my cheerleader mentality to that of a polished dancer, from a girl to a woman. I recognized my mother's quiet dignity in relation to a woman who continued to strive for an unattainable social niche.

At the starting gate of my career, I knew who I was—including limitations—and where I needed to go and how I intended to get there. Thanks Mom. Thanks Marilyn M. Fields.

***

During my mother's visit, Doug and his father swarmed around her as if she was the queen bee. She never met Doug's mother. Gene invited us to dinner at his home, not quite the mansion of his ex-wife, but Mom was impressed.

Only at night in bed—Doug graciously agreed to sleep on the couch in the living room—did Mom and I spend private time together.

"How do you feel about Gene?" It hadn't occurred to ask about my fiancé.

"Wonderful but painful."

I elbowed my body to a sitting position against the headboard and waited.

"It reminded me of the glamorous life style I once had."

"Are you interested in a second shot at it?"

"No. Just the opportunity to replay a memory of the Maloof's who gave my social status a little boost into the élite high society of Albuquerque." *Elite high society of Albuquerque* said tongue-in-cheek. "Of course there never was anything between us. My gosh, Dr. Peterson and I had already done quite well socially."

"You realize Gene is single, and he certainly is infatuated with you."

"I am happy with my friend Jim. I have Dr. Peterson's children and our grandchildren, and I have my two girls." She reached over and switched off the light on her side. "I wish you and Douglas all the best." She pulled the sheet tight to her chin. "I'll always be there for you." She rolled onto her side. "Even if the relationship doesn't work. Good night."

My turn to stare at the ceiling. I awoke to morning sun washing the light from my beside lamp.

***

With Doug's mother unavailable to us as a couple and my parents far off in different directions, Gene and I became close friends; too close for Doug's comfort, I discovered later. The three of us dined together quite often, and I pestered him for stories about his movie adventures.

Although Gene complained about playing a secondary role to Gordon MacRae in two back-to-back Rodgers and Hammerstein movies in the 1950's, he never sounded bitter. Anyone who saw *Oklahoma* could see that Gene was the better dancer, especially with his twirling rope routine. In the movie, *So This Is Paris*, he danced up a banister and over a Volkswagen.

"Please show me your dance steps by performing the routine with *Barysh*."

"That was 1954. Your Volkswagen was still scrap metal left over from the war." His chuckle turned serious. "If the movie is available at West Coast Video, rent a copy. I wouldn't mind seeing it myself."

I knew they carried *West Side Story*, but immediately buried that memory along with Jaime and *Limo Guy*. "Doug and I will check it out." We did, but none of the old classics had been copied to video.

Only after he was cheated from some *Oklahoma* royalties did he get a little excited.

"Why not sue?" I asked.

He modestly shrugged. "There were other opportunities."

When I had trouble finding jobs, Gene suggested the future for dancers was in Las Vegas, not a conversation Doug relished.

"If Vegas is so wonderful why isn't he there?" Doug expressed his resentment in the privacy of our apartment. "He'd never move away from movie and TV opportunities in Hollywood."

Doug filled me in on his father's *other opportunities.* Gene directed episodes of the original *Star Trek,* the first seasons of *I Dream of Jeannie, Gunsmoke, The Silent Force,* and *The San Pedro Beach Bums.* He directed the Elvis Presley films *Harum Scarum* and *Kissin' Cousins* for which he co-wrote the screenplay and received an award for best-written musical.

When I learned that he appeared with Buddy Ebsen in the NBC adventure series, I thought my association with celebrities had come full circle. I had no clue how many other celebrities were eagerly awaiting my rise to stardom, including Buddy Ebsen a second time.

Gene Nelson restored my faith in older men who would flatter but understood the boundaries of flirtation. Dancers rely entirely on their bodies to communicate yet enforce the rule *look-but-don't-touch. Break-it-you-own-it* does not apply to people.

I remained optimistic, but always in the back of my mind, *when you wake up with a hickey and a black eye, it is time to reevaluate the relationship.*

CHAPTER 13

Doug's father suggested I explore my dance career before we set our wedding date. "Give your relationship some time to develop. You've only known each other a few months." He had no clue why his son and I bonded so quickly.

After Doug and I spent a Christmas holiday with my family, Mom had no such reservations. Any young man willing to become baptized into her daughter's faith would make a good husband. Caroline had seen Doug's generous nature and agreed with Mom, until she and I had a chance to talk privately.

"Why haven't you set a date?" My sister's question startled me, almost as if I hadn't looked that far ahead. Doug had finally given up asking, and I thought the problem had gone away.

"I'm not sure we're getting married."

"You're wearing his ring. I think he is entitled to know if you intend to marry him."

"Oh, I plan to but...."

Caroline gave me her half-sister-half-mother glare.

"Now isn't a good time to make that kind of a decision." I told her about Doug's and my first squabble.

"Two people, no matter how much in love, will experience bumps along the way. Even you and I had our moments when we lived at home."

"But you're my sister. We know neither of us can run away from the relationship."

"Are you worried Doug might leave you some day?"

"Maybe it's the other way around."

"Sis, you better give this some serious thought."

I blurted, "I want to be a Las Vegas showgirl."

She shrugged. "If that's what you want, go for it."

"It's not what I want, it's my destiny." The source of my fantasy, not shared with anyone burst forth. "Gene Nelson, Doug's father, said, 'Mikel, you have the perfect body shape and personality to become a Las Vegas showgirl.'"

"Does Doug's father disapprove of your marrying his son?"

"I don't know. His mother for sure is against it."

"I guess you'll just have to go to Las Vegas and see if Doug follows you."

***

Shaken by my decision to move to Vegas, Doug graciously rented a van for all my stuff that no longer fit in *Barysh*. With our wedding plans on hold, we agreed that within three months, I would return, or he would move to be with me. We both knew he could never leave LA, and I felt for certain I would never go back. His father seemed excited for me, more than Doug did. Gene either saw the road bump that developed between me and his son—I could never hold back anything from Gene—or he seriously felt I was destined to be a showgirl. Doug objected, but he couldn't break free of parental influence, mother or father.

My second cousin on Dad's side, Venita, and her husband, Chava, invited me to stay with their family until I found a job, but Doug insisted we get a motel room for a couple of days. While he located storage rental for my furniture, I responded to an ad in the newspaper for dancers in the Can-Can Room. It sounded classical French with frilly costumes, bloomers, and colorful leggings. I walked in and backed away. Almost naked girls were humping a pole. Fortunately, one of the girls waiting her turn noticed my distress.

She said, "Honey, you need to check out the Hilton Showroom. I read in *Dirt Alert Paper* that they're opening auditions this week for their show, *Moulin Rouge de Paris*"

My first and second lesson; where to look for dance jobs and to pay attention to word of mouth. Although performers often compete for the same jobs, they support each other. I called the Hilton and set an appointment for the next day.

Doug and I picked up Mom at the airport; they had worked out that plan without me knowing, but I appreciated having her join us in my new adventure. She refused Doug's offer to pay for her motel room.

At the Hilton Hotel the next morning, while Doug asked directions to the auditorium, Mom pointed and said, "Look at that, Mikel."

Mom calling me by my stage name still felt strange. I had overlooked the life-sized cutout of Suzanne Somers. When I read, *Starring in Moulin Rouge de Paris*, my jaw dropped.

Doug joined us and handed me a brochure he had taken from the rack. "This is more current."

After Suzanne Somers he had written, *and Mikel Peterson.*

We entered the auditorium and a vast space opened surrounded with tiers of seats, over two thousand according to the brochure.

Mom paused at the back row. "You go ahead. Doug and I will watch from here."

I walked down the aisle and announced my arrival to a girl with a clipboard. She said, "Have a seat and we'll call you."

I had a chance to slow my racing heart and assess what dance moves would be required. The pirouette presented no problem, but when I heard, "Do your showgirl walk up and down stage," my heart skipped a beat. I might have the perfect shape, but, until that exact moment, I had no idea how to perform. I studied every nuance of the next couple of girls.

"Mikel Peterson."

I had all the steps in my head, and my legs obeyed my commands. I moved across the stage just like the others, and I felt satisfied with my performance. Had they expected better?

"Mikel, come down from the stage, please." I passed a row of disappointed faces and joined Walter Cartier in the house. "Love to have you in our show. We want you to dance topless."

"Topless? No way!"

I just turned down an offer from Walter Cartier of *Moulin Rouge de Paris*, one of the biggest shows in Vegas. In tears from insult, anger, or disappointment, I wasn't sure, I reported to Mom and Douglas.

Mom asked, "Does that mean you didn't get the job, even after that triple-whatever you did up on stage."

"I performed a perfect triple pirouette, and he offered me the job." A sniffle but no sob. "I turned it down. That guy wanted me to dance topless."

"This is Las Vegas, dear. You should have agreed."

I could not believe Mom's newfound ethics about nudity. "I won't chase after Walter Cartier and tell him *Mother* said it's okay to dance with my nipples staring back at the audience." Even after one of Cartier's dancers chased me up the aisle to convince me to stay, I just couldn't.

After Douglas returned to LA with the van, Mom treated me to dinner and the show I had turned down. She spent her last penny on me and had to have Jim wire her money to get back to Albuquerque.

I had considered going topless a slippery slope toward my red line. Jaime Rogers had asked me straight out to have sex. I rejected him, and he took away my Debbie Reynold's scholarship. I felt no regrets, but had my prudish attitude just destroyed an opportunity of a lifetime in Vegas? Jaime's voice reverberated. *It's time you face some hard facts about getting ahead in the entertainment industry.* Was the purpose of his assault merely to prepare me for this decision? I refused to dignify his bad behavior.

Dancers I talked to described the beauty and glamour of a naked body on stage, not the lust of sex. I realized that topless dancing was artful, certainly sensual but not overtly sexual. Patrons with that sordid taste visited the likes of the Can-Can Room. With my mother's consent, I gave in, and I kept my dignity. Mom understood the facts of life. What a hoot!

My second serious audition took place at the Flamingo for *City Lites.* I decided I would comply if the director wanted feathers sticking from every part of my body. Luckily, he did not. He offered me the part on the spot. I kept my cool, didn't *yippee* or anything, but when he stood to leave, like Detective Colombo on TV, he turned and said, "Oh, by the way. You *can* ice skate."

"Yes." Next time he saw me, I would be able to do a pirouette in ice skates or die trying.

"Do you have skates with you?"

"They're in storage." Holy crap. I never skated in my life, but I would have lied about still being a virgin, if it was important to get this job.

"I think we can round up a pair for you. What size street shoe do you wear?"

"Eight and a half." While I waited for the skates, I observed other dancers practicing the routine, skate across the ice and come to an abrupt 'T' stop. My learning style when asked to do something for a first time, I observe the moves and then perform as if I knew how.

Skates laced tight—*Mikel can do*—I stood, bent my knees, and mimicked other skaters' leg movements. I glided across the ice, and, executing the "T" stop, I kept balance.

Following an afternoon rehearsal, the dance captain brought me back stage to be fitted for costumes. In a whirlwind of color, I stood in my bra and panties with strangers, women thankfully, measuring, pinning, and tucking garments over my body, much like my mom in the privacy of the dressing room at Penny's Department Store.

In preparation for the early show, girls from the chorus line sat at tables applying makeup. Mirrors encircled with light bulbs left no blemish unnoticed. I rudely stared to learn how to make up my face. I had auditioned as an experienced showgirl, and when they headed to the stage, I felt quit sure my face would look like theirs when my time came.

Having completed rehearsals to the dance captain's satisfaction, I prepared for my first performance. That's when it hit me. I am a showgirl! In the dressing room, I only asked for help with the false eyelashes.

"I always seem to have trouble with these," I falsely confessed, and two girls came to my rescue. Butterflies disappeared the moment I held my pose and the curtain opened. I had found my niche.

With Mom on the phone the next morning, I thought she might have hung up before she finally asked, "Flamingo? The hotel that Bugsy Siegel built?"

"Yes, Mom. Somewhere back in the forty acres of gardens there is a Bugsy Siegel Memorial."

"That I want to see?"

"Before or after you watch me dance?" I decided to tease a little.

"Of course, I want to see your show. It's just that I remember when Bugsy Siegel was killed. What a shame. He was such a nice looking man, a movie star actually."

Mom had an eye for classy well-dressed men, and she was no slouch. I put aside a little from each paycheck to buy her a nice piece of jewelry.

Venita and Chava were wonderful, opening their home to my poodle and me. They became my second family away from home, first came Tyler and Camila in Van Nuys. When my poodle, *Nikov*—combined with *Barysh* spelled *Baryshnikov*—chewed the woodwork in my bedroom, Chava said, "It makes our house all-the-more lived in."

Nikov had been my second poodle from Douglas; the first was run over by a car while he was supposed to be watching her. That tragic accident contributed to our separation equally with Marilyn M. Fields' treatment of me as a future daughter-in-law, neither Doug's fault. Truth be told, I just fell out of love and tried to identify the cause. We could have patched an altercation that occurred, but I decided not to put forth the effort.

A harsh introduction to the desert sunshine, I dozed while tanning in Venita's backyard and suffered second-degree burns across my back and legs. Above the waist didn't matter so much, but I had to pull fishnet stockings over scorched legs and bottom. Despite throwing up and a high temperature, I made it through both performances that night, a sigh of relief when I unstrapped my bra for the late night topless act.

Douglas and I talked often over the phone, and he made a few uncomfortable visits. He came one last time to bring our relationship to a somewhat comfortable closure. He felt it would be too painful to watch me dance topless in *City Lites*, and I decided shacking up with him in a hotel room would be too dishonest.

Although Michael was merely an acquaintance at the time, Doug did not believe I had no serious boyfriend.

I had loved Doug; not only slept with him, but we woke up together, the true test of any relationship. I will always keep a warm spot in my heart for Douglas and for Stephen from back in high school.

The two years since leaving home had been highlighted by the 1984 Olympics and planning for a wedding, both in which I had a staring role. Unfortunately, each turned out to be temporary. In Vegas, I found a career that would last forever; at age twenty-one, the ten-year life span of a showgirl seemed like forever. What goes up must come down, and what goes up extremely high…. However, I would not trade that decade-long circus ride for anything.

Gene Nelson's telephone call changed my life.

CHAPTER 14

"Mikel, get to the MGM Grand and audition for *Jubilee*," Gene's phone conversation back in May of 1985, still crystal clear even after three decades of my fading memory. He mentioned Fluff, but not that he and others had already spoken to her about me.

I checked my outdated copy of *Dirt Alert Paper*, but the news hadn't yet reached that issue. Unsure if someone named Fluff really existed, I called the box office for details, as if I intended to purchase tickets. Fluff LeCoque was the production manager of *Jubilee* and the woman gave me the correct spelling of her last name.

When I asked if auditions were being held, she said, "Come on down at two this afternoon." She sighed. "Why didn't you say you were a showgirl? I used to be one myself."

Retirement jobs for older performers had yet to enter my consciousness. My bigger concern was the extra weight from taking birth control pills since my time with Douglas, but no immediate need. I dressed in tight black slacks and a close-fitting blouse, and of course, my performance shoes.

Jubilee Theater arched above the single door to the auditorium almost as if it was a tucked–away theater. The *Celebrity Room* I mistakenly went to first seemed bigger. Even with the house lights dimmed, it had the feel of luxurious intimacy.

"Mikel Peterson, we don't have your name on the list."

I deflected a jolt of fear with optimism. "I only heard about the auditions this morning. I would really like to try out." I held back telling him that I waited my entire life to be a showgirl now that I settled the issue of topless dancing.

"We have our quota, girls who signed up ahead of time."

From stage, a woman my mother's age and just as beautiful, declared, "Mikel Peterson," as if she knew me. "Come on up here and get in line." The world stood still as I followed the yellow brick road to the opportunity of a lifetime. Almost on cue, Fluff LeCoque, I assumed, said, "Observe the yellow line. Don't ever step behind it."

Seemed arbitrary to me, the vast stage as wide as a football field continued back at least to the fifty-yard line. Later, I learned that the area behind the yellow line could drop from sight and that in the history of *Jubilee* one tragic fall occurred.

Fluff positioned my body at the end of the line and whispered, "*Those guys* who recommended you have no say in your being accepted as a showgirl in *Jubilee*. I will decide that."

Who else of Gene's entourage spoke for me? His final words, "We'll be rooting for you," I thought meant family, but could it have been David L. Wolper or Ron Field from the '84 Olympics? It was not the sort of question I could ask my friend, just show my appreciation and not let him down.

Fluff not only ruled out special treatment, but she added, "You will either fit the part or not get the job." *Fit*, not *perform?*

I was confused until anonymous comments came through the darkened house. The few of us who were not already smiling were told to do so.

"Number two's face is too round, that nose on number seven…, the chin on number six!" A loud clear masculine voice, "Take off your tops." My decisive moment and I proudly displayed that part me usually reserved for intimacy. "Shoulders back, perk your boobs up, turn around slowly."

Fluff ordered, "Miss Palm, take them through the basic moves and we'll see how well they follow."

I felt Fluff's eyes glued to me as if I had dared to challenge some time-honored tradition. Our dance captain, Diane Palm, directed us through a few coordinated steps.

After some background mumbling, "Number nine!" My number-nine heart skipped a beat. "Walk upstage and back onto the apron." I told my feet what to do and my legs not to buckle. When I reached the yellow line, I turned and felt a surge of optimism, my stride never before so confident.

More mumbling and I held my breath.

"Go to the top of the stairs and come down."

Dumbfounded, I glanced back toward the darkened area stage right and a lighted staircase had emerged behind the yellow line.

Continued mumbling, which I interpreted as a good thing.

"Go back to the office to sign papers and pick up your rehearsal instructions."

I glanced from the dance captain to Fluff. "I got the Job? Really?"

"You can start rehearsals." Fluff's expression remained unchanged. "I decide if you *really* get the job."

Dazed and confused, I staggered up the aisle and into a world of lights blinking, bells tingling, and coins reverberating against metal catch basins. I approached an elderly woman feeding dollars into a slot machine with a gloved hand.

I asked, "Do you know where the office is?" A methodic pull of the handle, and she gestured with her head what could have been any direction.

"I'll take you there." A scantly clad girl with a tray full of empty glasses and a name tag that read, *Hi, I'm Susan from Wyoming* paused to make eye contact.

I got in step with her. "I just got hired as a showgirl."

"That's nice. On a good night, I'll make more money and I only have to show cleavage."

She reminded me of my days back at The Daisy. I said, "You work hard for your money, and I respect that."

"Thanks."

***

I hadn't included my dancing experience at the Flamingo on my resume for fear it may hinder my chances, like not stealing talent, which, I learned later, is often what showrooms did. Besides, Fluff probably knew I danced in *City Lites* and wanted to see how I handled my transition to *Jubilee*.

I will never know to what extent Gene Nelson had dealt me a winning hand. Nor would I ever know to what extent my appearance versus my talent contributed to my earning the part. Mouths and lips required a certain shape; all faces had to have a vertical structure, so cruelly demonstrated years later in the movie, *Showgirls*. Many dancers objected to Elizabeth Berkley's portrayal of a showgirl in that 1995 movie, but watching it, I recalled being tossed into a meat-market atmosphere and how depersonalized I felt. Once hired, unfortunately, girls' egos often soared at the cost of manners and common decency. I made it a point to treat the wardrobe women and stagehands with respect, even the stagehands who guffawed while we did some costume changes in their presence.

I gave a two-week notice and offered to stay on until a replacement could be found, continued dancing nightly at the Flamingo, while memorizing the dance steps for *Jubilee* during daytime rehearsals. Showrooms at the Flamingo and Bally's went dark on different days, so I attended a *Jubilee* performance on my night off.

Deep shades of red permeated plush seating and velvety curtains. In place of box seats on either side, curtains outlined false doors and windows hiding small mechanical stages that dropped from the ceiling. Sitting in an audience and facing the *Ziegfeld* Stage from the *Jubilee* showroom was an overwhelming experience.

From the time the live orchestra intoned the performance from the pit and the curtain opened, I sat mesmerized. The beauty, glamour, and talent of the dancers, male and female, took my breath away. The stage transformed itself to enhance the theme of ten different songs and stories within the music, each requiring costume changes. Diane Palm led the *Water Fountain* dance pattern, each costume adorned with five thousand feathers. The dazzling array of ten thousand Swarovski crystal rhinestones—six-hundred-and-sixty-six on each vest of the nineteen male dancers—and fifty showgirls in full array both on stage and catwalk above the audience brought *Jubilee* to a climax. I refused to get up and leave.

A sympatric usher said, "There's always an empty seat near the back. I'll take you there just before the curtain opens for the late performance."

I envisioned myself performing topless as a *Jubilee* dancer. Little did I realize how many, additional wonders I would encounter before the curtain opened on my first performance. The shock of it came in stages. We began in smaller groups doing segments of the show, new girls blended with seasoned dancers. I was amazed at how well we were accepted, considering that some girls had been called in for a rehearsal they may not have needed. My most lasting relationships began with those groups of new and seasoned dancers.

After a second or third rehearsal in segments, Diane Palm gestured for me to approach. "Mikel, follow me downstairs to be fitted for costumes." A tinge of panic rippled up-and-down my spine, not having shed those couple extra pounds I tried to hide during the audition.

We went down three levels of stairs to the basement stage left, and walked along a concrete-lined hallway bypassing the pit occupied with all the heavy lifting machinery, to the area under front stage ahead of the yellow line.

Diane paused and pointed. "There's another staircase up ahead for dancers entering the set from stage right, and up one more level is a small dressing area. When costumes changes are allotted only ten seconds, it has to be done back stage."

"In front of the stage crew?"

"You'll get used to it. They already are."

We turned a corner into a burst of light and color and a beehive of activity. Down a row of mirror-backed tables, girls peered at their reflections between and around a veil of wigs, headdresses, bras, and g-strings dangling from overhead shelves jammed with frilly and feathery apparel. A powdery fragrance punctuated by the acetate of nail polish blended into an aroma that I considered nauseatingly delicious. I stood in awe.

Diane gave a backhanded wave. "Nudes' stations are ahead. Those were the Bluebells. Their costumes are uniquely different."

And more extensive, I would have guessed; *only different*, I learned later. Covering breasts doesn't mean more things to put on.

"Get undressed down to panties, and put your clothes in this locker." She wafted her hand, took a few steps, and pointed to a chair midway down the second line of tables. "This will be your station in the short nudes' area." Bare breasted girls sat on either side applying make-up for the early show.

I stood at my locker naked—so it seemed—when Fluff stepped out of her office. "Mikel! You have gained weight since the audition." She jabbed her finger toward the scale set out in plain view. "Get over here and on the scale this minute."

I tensed my abs, as if that would make a difference, and stepped onto the dreaded platform.

Fluff's jaw dropped. "You loose 16 pounds in two and a half weeks or you're out of here. Not one pound less!"

A wall of girls' heads appeared, one atop the other, peering out from a row of dressing stations. Diane said, "We may as well wait to fit your costumes."

Shamed, I opened my locker to retrieve my clothes, but changed my mind. "I want to check out my dressing table." Head raised, I walked to the vacant spot and addressed the girls on either side of me. "Hi. I'm Mikel. I'll be joining you in a couple of weeks."

I got a couple of weak greetings, and then the girl with *Lisa* glued to her mirror said, "Good for you, Mikel."

I fretted, as I stood outside the stage back door where my friend, Michael Lekar, agreed to meet me. *Barysh* had been a bit under the weather lately, and I awaited Dad's answer to my *please help* call.

Michael returned a sympathetic ear to my weight problem— after he chuckled—as I felt his pain from recently losing his fiancé in a plane crash. I met him at her family's jewelry store when I went to buy Mother's birthday present. I had finally reached a financial level with some discretionary funds, until *Barysh* gave his threatening burp.

"You can do it, Mikel." Michael's tone reeked with false hope.

"I will do it," I sobbed.

"That's losing over a pound a day."

"I have a secret strategy."

He didn't even mention our planned dinner that evening, just a quiet ride home. "You going to share your secret strategy?"

"I'm off the pill immediately, limit my food intake to three pieces of fruit a day, and extra time at the gym when not in rehearsals."

"Sounds to me like I just lost another girlfriend."

"I could never replace your fiancé. We'll just be friends."

Fluff allowed me to continue rehearsals, but kept a suspicious eye on me—my body mostly. She probably wondered if my shedding pounds was the result of cocaine use.

My next eye-opener occurred when interacting with mechanized stage machinery, still one segment of the show at a time. We danced on and around massive constructions elevated from below stage, battens lowered through T-track counterweight systems, and huge pieces of set shoved in from the wings.

The activity on and off set boggled my mind. Stay out of the way, my first rule and choreograph each step off stage as precisely as Donn Arden had me follow on stage. No improvising during performance or short cuts between scenes. With all female dancers, more than half of them topless, rubbing shoulders with about as many stagehands moving props around, one would think there would be embarrassing encounters. I marveled at the self-control of those guys, not the male dancers who were mostly gay, but the stage crew who were either too busy or just used to bare breasted women getting in their way.

There must have been a dozen elevators raising and lowering huge construction pieces like the Titanic's engine room, deck, and grand salon, the iceberg, the Philistine Palace, and multiple staircases and platforms to accommodate scores of dancers.

The dressing room just moments before a performance buzzed with costume changes, approximately one wardrobe woman for three female dancers, the men generally dressed themselves. A weird feeling with someone positioning your breasts in their halters while a headgear lowers and attaches to your body. At least fishnets and g-strings were our own responsibility, as was face and body makeup.

With my opening dance costume still a tight fit, Fluff didn't ask me to step on a scale. Only later did I realize how significant her oversight had been. One pound over and she would have had no choice but to stick to her word and release me.

My first *Jubilee* performance occurred June 28, 1985, and I was hyped. Between shows, the short nudes in my group insisted I take a break, but I wanted to stay on and review some of the steps. Fortunately, the stagehands kicked us off so they could repair the Titanic and prepare for the late show. To me, the sinking of the Titanic was minor compared with what would take place during my second performance, displaying my bare breasts in front of the showroom filled to capacity. To me, *City Lites* had been my junior varsity-team experience.

I went through the late show not once distracted by my naked-ness, even after one of the girls filled me in on showgirls' little secret. "Harden your nipples."

After my first night's performance, Michael treated me to a late dinner with a glass of Champagne. He took me home. His home. My overactive Gemini brought Michael and me together at a vulnerable time in our lives. Each of us was saddened over the ending of an intimate relationship, his loss unbelievably tragic. Sympathy may have contributed to my attraction to him, but he became the white knight who rode into my life when I needed support. In addition, he took responsibility for birth control.

Although my feelings for him were genuine, his physical appearance and personality contributed to my infatuation. In the back of my mind, I kept looking for the ideal partner to give me a beautiful child. In a glamorous profession like show business, it is hard not to make relationship decisions based on such criteria, and choices relying on the immediate personal needs often become a temporary refuge. So it was with Michael and me. We discussed marriage from time to time, but mostly we drifted to a point never less than good friends.

CHAPTER 15

Sour-faced and arms crossed, Fluff stood backstage after the late-show curtain dropped. "All nudes, rehearsal tomorrow at one o'clock. You were terrible tonight." Groans in unison from the girls, each looking to see who missed a step.

Lisa whispered in my direction, "Don't fret, sweetie. It wasn't you or any of us. Fluff just does that to keep us on our toes." A friend for life, I decided.

Satisfied with wrecking everyone's afternoon plans, Fluff cut across the stage toward the exit.

"No consideration for anyone with day jobs," grumbled the girl who apparently had one. I had been still looking.

The men's dance captain approached me. "Mikel. You got a minute?"

"Yeah, sure Joe." First name basis came easy with the female dancers and most of the men, but Joe McDonough seemed a bit distant. However, he called me Mikel, and I responded in kind.

"You'll be here tomorrow afternoon." A question or a statement of fact, I couldn't tell.

I nodded and he imitated the gesture as in sympathetic understanding. "You guys don't have much choice."

I nodded again, he continuing to agree.

"Are you familiar with MGM Grand Business Theater?"

"No, I'm not." I resisted shaking my head. "I imagine it's part of the same company that holds our performance contracts."

"Exactly, a spin-off." He blushed. "I'm the director."

Of the various part-time jobs dancers held, a position in MGM Grand's management sounded impressive.

"One of my clients would like to observe you and some others perform. Just by chance, tomorrow's rehearsal would be an ideal time for him to sit in."

"Fluff..." I glanced in the direction she had exited as if her trail were still visible.

"Don't worry. Business Theater is part of our parent company, so there would be no conflict of interest." He sensed my concern. "I'll be here in case the guy from Sherman Williams wants to see if we click together."

"Sherman Williams? The paint company?"

"Yeah, we're doing their promotional show, and you'd be just perfect." He demonstrated a little jazz step and hummed a few bars of "Singing in the Rain." Baffled, I didn't respond by voice or gesture.

"It's the tune we'll be dancing to. A commercial for their water-proof products. That's what Business Theater is all about." Breaking eye contact, "I told him about you and he's eager to see you perform."

Bursting to accept, I didn't want to sound desperate.

"I hope you don't mind."

"Mind!" All caution to the wind. "I would love to do the show."

"Good. We'll see you tomorrow."

***

The next morning, I knocked on my neighbor's door, and Willie greeted me, his smile peeking through gray stubble. I threw my arms around him, inhaling the comforting aromas of Brylcreem mingling with steam from cabbage simmering on the stove. "I found my day job."

"Good for you. Now you come for lunch more often. No time to cook at home."

Willie retired from Ringling Brothers Circus as an acrobat, the first to climb four levels on a shoulder-to-shoulder people-stack. He thrilled me with tales of the good old circus days. I would share my day's adventure with him, and he'd magically recreate his three-ring circus straight from the nineteen-thirties, animals, acrobats, clowns, and all. I explained in detail the events of my previous night.

"Your friend dances with you and is a program director, too?" His eyes widened.

"He's the men's dance captain. I didn't even think he knew who I was."

"You hang on to him." He scowled. "He isn't gay, is he?"

"Come on, Willie. Not all dancers are gay."

***

After doing a few shows with Joe McDonough, a wave of anxiety spread through the *Jubilee* cast. MGM had sold its hotel, casino, and showroom to Bally's, a slot machine manufacturing company. From our point of view, the transaction remained seamless, although momentarily stressful. The hotel's reputation suffered from the fire that killed eighty-four people three years earlier, but our show in the *Ziegfeld* Room continued to be its greatest asset.

News that *Jubilee* would continue under new ownership relieved us of worries, but under which corporate entity would Business Theater function? Bally's prevailed, but it was difficult for clients to use the new name. Joe McDonough continued as director for a few months until Corporate brought in a new face and talent, someone who sang and wrote lyrics.

Joe Morris, who performed in Reno, immediately made some changes. Our usual group reported to the *Ziegfeld* Showroom to audition for his Ford Industrial commercial, an extravaganza that probably cinched his role as the new director. From up on the stage, Joe introduced himself and described Business Theater to any of us in the front rows who might be auditioning for the first time.

Spreading his arm, he said, "In a few weeks, this area will be filled with industrial equipment with the Titanic boiler room as a backdrop. Until then, we'll use our imagination and some mock pieces of equipment to block our choreography."

He put the dancers through a few of his sequences selected a dozen of us, calling my name for the lead role. Worried how some of the more seasoned dancers might feel, I was careful not to gloat.

Thus, began my eight-year relationship with Joe Morris managing Bally's Business Theater. Over that span, he negotiated multiple productions with more than thirty companies, hired the talent as needed, and located the appropriate space for each production. Ford Industrial was the only company set up on the *Ziegfeld* stage, most others in Bally's Convention Hall and some at various venues around Vegas. It was my favorite.

According to Joe, the company rep always requested me. "Make sure you have the blond with the wide smile lead the dance sequence." After my first audition, Joe never put me through the process again, often asked me to participate in the selection of other dancers.

We danced to familiar Broadway musicals with lyrics rewritten to enhance a product or a company. For instance, to the Sherman Williams' commercial, Joe added the catchy phrase, *paint it, splash it, wash it* repeated as a refrain. In the annual SIA tradeshow at Bally's Convention Center, we dressed in fashionable skiwear suitable for a Denver winter, not summer in Vegas, quite a contrast to g-string and fishnet later that same day.

With Dunlap Tires, we danced in cowboy boots, jeans, and western shirts to music from *Oklahoma*. Gene Nelson, I did that one just for you.

Some of the other borrowed musicals included, *Sound of Music*, *Grease*, *Babes in Toyland*, *Hello Dolly*, and *Cabaret*. Video Industrial Company produced two of my most memorable performances, one my impersonation of Ginger Rogers and one of Marilyn Monroe. Joe rented Ginger Rogers' dress worn in her movie *One Hundred Stars* when she danced with Fred Astaire. I never before or since felt fabric that smooth on my skin. The other time I was made up as Marilyn Monroe.

I idolized these two women for their beauty and their talent and modeled my life after theirs except for divorces, Ginger five and Marilyn three, perhaps the reason I never married.

One production just for entertainment with no special endorsement occurred in Bally's Celebrity Room midway through Super Bowl XXI between the New York Giants and the Denver Broncos. At half time, the TV projection screen was raised, and we preempted the televised showgirl performance live on stage. No one complained about missing the thousand dancers in the Rose Bowl Stadium.

Although we often danced as showgirls in Business Theater productions, the culture was quite different from *Jubilee*, more informal including direct interaction with the audience. As our title implied, attendees were business people, men mostly, rather than tourists who bought tickets to be awed and then headed back home to shock friends with the nude dancing they had seen.

During a road show to Miami, Joe introduced me as a dancer from the '84 Olympics. A client recognized me from my picture back then on the front page of the *Miami Herald*. He brought me his copy the next day. I remembered doing my stretch exercises under the Olympic arches but not that a photographer had taken my picture. Had I known, I would have put on a real show, might have pulled a muscle and missed the entire Olympics.

***

Fluff's relentless drive for perfection kept our performance fine-tuned, but it encouraged opposing personality temperaments, competitive and cooperative. Everyone wanted to excel and be rewarded, but many of us regarded peer acceptance as important as achievement. I never tried to outdo the girl next to me, but rather helped both of us become the best we can. This attitude brought positive results on stage and backstage. My personality tends more toward social than prima donna.

I tried to befriend everyone, and I treated my coworkers with respect. A few of the performers looked down on the twenty-some wardrobe women or the wig lady, not just tall nudes who physically had to peer down at most people, perhaps the reason they appeared more austere than us short nudes even off stage.

A simple *thank you* to the person who spent hours repairing the feathers on my costume always produced a smile. A *good job* to my dance mates heading back to our dressing areas reduced stress in all of us. Pointing out an occasional miss-step during a performance should be Fluff's responsibility to identify and correct, not the other dancers. She could have been more kind with her comments, because some of the girls were so sensitive. Sobs heard off stage were quite common, and I always tried to console Fluff's victims.

I seldom cried throughout my career, an abrupt change with Mom in hospice.

Dancing should be physically exhausting, and some performers dragged themselves off stage and home to bed. I found it exhilarating. I would finish with as much energy as I began each performance. I had enough sense to go home, if a job awaited me the next day, but more often than not, a party at one of the nightclubs until wee hours of the morning tweaked my interest. *Networking* justified my carousing, opportunities encountered through social interactions. I never gambled and drank very little, although showgirls seldom had to pay for a cocktail. I needed to keep my wits about me, Vegas being a wild and often unforgiving place.

A couple of us *Jubilee* showgirls stopped at Botany's Night Club after the late show, and I caught a glimpse of Steve Kostov at a table with his usual cadre of admirers. A flash memory from The Daisy erupted into panic no less traumatic than that night in his bedroom.

I whispered, "Let's get out of here."

Questioned why the sudden rush to leave, I considered who would be only slightly less scary than Kostov. "Didn't you see the Spilotro brothers standing at the bar?" *Anthony the Ant* Spilotro and his brother Mickey sometimes hung out at Botany's and would hit on us.

Later that year, a federal grand jury in Los Angeles summoned me to testify against Steve Kostov being charged with burning down a friend's drycleaner business to collect the insurance. My mother sent a letter to the judge asking to excuse me from court, because I would lose my job as *a Jubilee* Showgirl. Kostov got what he deserved. No less deserving, the mob beat up the Spilotro brothers and buried them alive in June of that year.

I felt safest at parties on the lake in broad daylight, and they were the most fun. Businessmen tended to be more direct than show biz people with their *making moves on me* and more accepting of my *turndown*. Most of them just wanted to be around beautiful young women, and who was I to deprive them.

One time a Playboy scout approached me to do a photo-shoot for a feature story on *showgirls*. I rejected the offer because Donn Arden was extremely sensitive about any of his performers accepting jobs borrowing the *Jubilee* concept, Business Theater being the exception. Outside careers were permissible and sometimes necessary to pay the bills. I auditioned with Jackie Baskow Talent Agency for a few jobs, which didn't interfere with Donn Arden's code. After I left *Jubilee*, I eagerly pursued many other opportunities, but the *Playboy* scout never returned for me

CHAPTER 16

In line with the other short nudes, tall nudes dispersed behind us, entire cast caught in that split-second pose before breaking into the finale number, *The Don Arden Walk*, to the music, "It's a Hollywood Jubilee," came an ear-shattering phone interruption. I sat up instantly alert, prepared to receive the dreaded call from hospice.

"Hello." A brief dial tone, a click, and silence. My precious dream, one I hadn't experienced since Caroline and I placed Mom in assisted living, interrupted by someone fingering the wrong buttons on their cell phone. Pre-dawn just weeks before Christmas, 2014, thoughts of sugarplums weren't dancing in my head. Why would Mom, so near death, allow this dream to occupy my sleep, or had it been her intention to distract me from my sadness? I'll mention it to her and maybe get a flick of an eyelid in response.

Since hospice, Mom mostly occupied my dream-state to communicate when she could no longer speak, along with cloud patterns and bird formations, and, on rare occasions, whispering into my ear when I am half-awake. *Tell it as it really happened, Mikel*, her approval for me to bare all secrets?

Yes, Mom, before curtain opened, we nudes moistened fingers and rubbed our nipples to make then stand out, and Dad agreed my going topless was no big deal after he got over his shock when I forewarned him.

His reaction, "You're still my carefree little girl splashing in our backyard kiddies' pool."

Nudes often chuckled over our parents' reactions to our dancing topless.

The toughest hurdle for me to overcome, other than losing weight on short notice, was my limited experience with ballet, not my mother's fault. She enrolled me in ballet classes as well as flamingo dance with castanets, but I preferred frilly dresses to petticoats and tutus. I hadn't developed ballet-hardened toes, and when Jeff, a dance partner, set me down a bit hard, I broke my pinkie. Three years later, he was even tougher on my body and my career—he gave me a son. Losing *Jubilee*, not Jeff's fault or mine, hurt more than anything else in my career, but having Nicholas in my life made up for my loss ten times over.

Caroline started medical school in California about the time I moved to Las Vegas, but a three-hundred-mile separation presented a financial hurdle neither of us could readily overcome. However, Mom—probably our friend Jim—bought airline tickets for her and Caroline to watch me perform in *City Lites* and once again in *Jubilee*. Later, Jim came to Vegas alone, and Caroline drove here a few times with girlfriends to show off her *fabulous* sister. I reveled in the attention.

About a year into my *Jubilee* experience Dad, and his fiancée, Judy, flew to Vegas to get married and take in my show. At the airport, he jammed their luggage into *Barysh's* front trunk and half of the back seat.

He shook his head. "You still driving your VW from high school days?"

"Please, Dad. His name is *Barysh*, and he's a bit sensitive about his age."

"Like your father? Maybe it's time to put him out to pasture."

Who, Dad or *Barysh*? I bit my tongue.

The next day we visited a Chevrolet dealership, and Dad signed the finance papers. When I thanked him, he said, "You get to make the payments."

I told him the new Hyundai Excels cost less than the used Chevy Camaro he picked out, and he said, "So do the Yugos, but they are both foreign junk." Personally, I felt guilty about not buying a Ford considering my role in promoting that company's brand. Today, I drive a four-year-old 2010 Red Camaro with *SHOWGRL* vanity plate. Father still knows best.

That night at *Jubilee*, he saw my breasts for the first time since I was a child. It proved to be less shocking than he thought it would be.

I finger-waved and winked to my friends in the audience, pointing out ahead of time which of my ten sets of dances to pay special attention. If Fluff had noticed when she periodically critiqued us from the audience without warning, I would have heard her call, "Into my office, now!"

Only dancers feared Fluff's wrath, so I bribed David, a stagehand, to take pictures of me from the sidelines during a performance, an action that could have both of us fired. We became good friends, until he invited me to his apartment. He had papered his walls with my photos, promotional head and body shots.

"You're sick!" probably not the best thing to say under the circumstances, but my reaction startled him. "Take them down right now." I waited until he handed them over before I walked out. He apologized later, but his obsession with me didn't end. Most of the camera, light, and stage crewmembers reacted professionally around beautiful scantily clad women, maybe a second glance or possibly a snicker when we quick-changed in their presence back stage. I realized David's glance my way was more of a stare.

After the late show, those of us without spouses or day jobs often met at one of the all-night clubs to let off steam. Some of the girls gambled and a few drank a bit too much, but I saved my money, enough to buy a condominium after I returned from the '88 Pre-Olympics in Korea. One night some of us girls checked the action at the Shark Club, out of costume but quite apparent who we were and where we just came from. David tagged along and became possessive, following me around and stationed himself at the end of the booth to lock me in.

I purposely moved through the crowd, not seriously flirting but enjoying its effect on some of the men, demonstrating to David and others that we were not a couple. He stomped out of the club. In the morning, I found scratches across my new-to-me-car from Dad.

The next day, I went directly back stage before getting dressed for the show. (Undressed, actually, but we did have to slip into g-string and fishnet stockings.) "Did you key my car?"

"Yeah. You ignored me and tantalized every fellow in the place. I was mad at you."

"You pay for the paint job and, from now on, leave me alone, or I will report the damage to the police and charge you with stalking me." I would have threatened to get him fired, but he could report that I had pictures of a *Jubilee* performance. We came to an uncomfortable truce.

Male-female interactions in show biz are quite different from other workplaces. Since we had few straight men to flirt with, like little girls playacting with dollies, the nude dancers dressed the gay guys in female costumes with full makeup and let them imitate our dance steps. Some of us would pretend to be Fluff and critique them from the audience. Many of them would have been tough competition if they had boobs.

In another world, they would have been teased, but everything is topsy-turvy in showgirl culture. The guys who didn't participate earned the raspberries. I felt sorry for my partner who usually was picked on. Jeff had a magical, almost prince charming physique, blond, blue eyes, masculine yet agile. In his late thirties, he had to exercise hard to stay limber. Whenever he threatened to quit and sell real estate back in California, I encouraged him to stay with the dance company. Subconsciously, I probably considered him as a candidate to give me a child, but I was not ready to be a mom just then. I remained neutral to the possibility, open to the idea if it was meant-to-be. My philosophy, fate presents opportunities, and I latch onto the good stuff.

With steady income from *Jubilee*—four hundred dollars a week plus fifty dollars extra for going topless, twenty-five for each boob—Rachael Davies, a lead principal from England, and her husband, Eric, invited me to share expenses on their two bedroom apartment. I hadn't shared an apartment with anyone that I hadn't slept with, Douglas Nelson the only one up to that time. A fellow dancer, Tricia, knew some wealthy boat owners who enjoyed spicing up their parties with beautiful girls clad in g-strings only, tan lines were strictly taboo on stage.

Speeding across Lake Mead, hair blown in the wind while dancing on deck, we were the picture of life in the fast lane. On nights that *Jubilee* went dark, party houseboats, windows aglow and music echoing off the canyon walls, cruised the smooth dark waters. Glamorous on stage, vibrant and alive off, showgirls, at least most of us, tasted the good life. Comfortable in our skins, we presented a look-but-don't-touch image, intimacy reserved for special relationships.

After a late show, Fluff called me to her office. "Do you own a formal evening gown?"

"Yes." Buying nice clothes was my only extravagance.

"Tomorrow at the regular time, report directly to the hotel lobby dressed for dinner. You won't be in the show."

"What...?" Over two thousand performances and I never missed a night.

"Don't tell anyone, but you're meeting a special hotel guest."

I heard stories from the early fifties where topless dancers were actually required to gamble, drink, and 'accompany' the VIPs in the casinos after shows. When Margaret Kelly (*Miss Bluebell*) brought *Bluebell Showgirls* from England to Las Vegas in 1958, she set the precedent that her dancers did not join members of the audience, nor do they uncover their breasts. Donn Arden reintroduced topless dancing in *Jubilee*, but the rule against customer mingling remained in place, so I thought.

Diane Palm, our captain who knew every dance position, would replace me, or seven dancers would spread to fill in for the missing girl, if I called in sick, which actually should have been the case. Fluff could spot an ounce of fat on a girl's belly from a mile off, but she hadn't noticed my runny nose.

In the hotel lobby, I joined a gathering of chic ladies trying to act casual while their escorts out on the casino floor placed one last bet on the *roll of the dice*.

"Mikel, you are just as stunning off stage." I held my showgirl smile to avoid my gaping mouth when George Peppard appeared. "Thank you for agreeing to join me for dinner."

Fortunately, I lost my voice and said nothing, which was the correct non-response to maintain an air of mystery. Otherwise, I might have said something stupid like, "The pleasure's all mine." or maybe even asked for an autograph, which he freely offered days later in the Celebrity Room. George opened the crux of his elbow, so I placed a white-gloved hand on his forearm. I cooched my legs and slowly turned my head nearly face-to-face, my makeup just enough *showgirl* so everyone recognized his date as such. "Thank you." Off we pranced to exquisite dining.

George ordered champagne, we toasted the show, and I sipped. He ordered for both of us, our meals arrived in multiple stages, and after a barrage of questions, he said, "Mikel, you're not eating."

I couldn't deny it, so I remained quiet.

"I think you are not well."

His first clue, tissues from my clutch-purse dabbing my nose, although the job required my table napkin. "I have a bit of a cold," I confessed. "I only hope I'm not contagious."

"That would be unfortunate, with my audition tomorrow." A sympathetic, slightly embarrassed expression, "Perhaps I should fetch you a taxi."

"I'm sorry," I squeaked, and I am still sorry for the wasted opportunity. Not that I might have stepped across my red line, I regret the evening had not played itself out. George Peppard was a gentleman, and he merely wanted a *Pretty Woman* for company, I think.

I steeped some herbal tea and soaked my wretched body in a steamy bath chuckling to myself, "Not up to par for an evening with George Peppard."

Throughout my *Jubilee* career, I got along with members of the cast, treating the girls as sisters. I encountered only one minor conflict with my dance captain. We ran a pattern shaping a water fountain, and she hit me on the back with her fan, probably an accident. From the audience, we looked like two giant birds vying for a breadcrumb. When it happened again, I became confused. A third time, *three strikes and you are out*, screamed the Gemini umpire in my head.

I confronted her downstairs outside Fluff's office. "Don't you ever hit me in the back again. I know you're doing it on purpose." All the tall nudes who walked by cheered, because she had been doing similar things to them. I didn't know if she was just bored, or needed to show authority, or wanted a reaction. She panicked, knowing I befriended the directors and managers—my personal goal to earn the approval of men who made all the decisions.

Later we talked in Help's Hall between shows, and she admitted to personal problems, mostly with a sister. I accepted her as a person, and we became friends.

After twenty-nine years with *Jubilee*, Fluff LeCoque, age eighty, retired, and Diane Palm officially became stage manager, a well-earned reward for years of diligence and hard work. Three years later, November 19, 2013, Fluff was inducted into the *Show Biz Friends Hall of Fame*, and all of us former and present showgirls were invited to the bash. By all indications, she will outlive my mother.

I experienced some unsettling moments during my *Jubilee* years. I had three wisdom teeth pulled in the morning and replaced bloody gauze between shows that night. Once, while running across stage with a big tambourine, I hit the side drop and fell. Sampson, his focus locked on Delilah, tripped and fell on top a table in the audience.

He said "Hi,' to the startled couple and jumped back onto the stage.

An overhead light dropped barely missing me. Ricky grabbed a broom and danced it onto the stage, sweeping up the shattered glass while in step with the music. He will always hold a special spot in my heart as one of my many friends who died of HIV/*AIDS*. Always, the show went on.

Accidents happened, but when a split-second lapse in my mental tape-recorder occurred, I became concerned. I immediately caught up with the other seven dancers, and I doubt people in the audience noticed. Dance steps become second nature, but we have to remember each performance is a first time to that night's audience. Fortunately, it never happened to me again.

"How's it going, Baby?" I turned to face Dean Martin, martini glass in hand, coming down the stairs followed by his bodyguard. Dressed in street clothes between shows, I lifted my showgirl-made-up-face minus the eyelashes and headgear, poised as if ready for the curtain to open, and responded, "I'm doing great."

His greeting was classic Dean Martin from his comedy show Mom allowed Caroline and me to watch with her when we were still in grade school. Too bad Mom was back in Albuquerque. I could hardly wait to call and tell her.

Dean Martin had been the starring act for the Celebrity Room's Grand Opening on December 23, 1973, and he did many more since then. When not performing, he and his Rat Pack paraded on-and-off stage to wow the audience, and us showgirls. We were always welcomed in the Celebrity Room, and management didn't consider it a breach of the rule not to mingle.

Included in my personal collection from Celebrity Room encounters are pictures of Dean as well as Sylvester Stallone, Wayne Newton, Jerry Lewis, Tom Jones, Righteous Brothers, Robert Goulet, Mel Tellis, Sam Kenison, Kenny Rogers, and Sammy Davis, Jr. Dozens more when I hadn't a camera, which was not often.

Showgirls often attract undesirable attention, men loitering outside the backstage door hoping for a naked dancer to step out for a breath of fresh air. We never left the stage without first covering our bodies, but I had to walk that gauntlet on the way to the parking lot at the end of the night. One time, a man in a convertible pulled up alongside, one hand on the wheel and one on his erection. The stage door had locked behind me, so I had no option but to run to my car, lock myself in, and hope he wouldn't follow me home. Safely in my apartment, my fear turned to rage.

The next day, I complained to the management about the performers' lack of security, knowing nothing would be done.

Back during my training period, a mother and junior-high-school daughter confronted me as I parked *Barysh* in the employee lot.

When I rolled down the window, the woman raised her fist and yelled, "Hey, you cut me off, back there."

"I'm sorry." My apology should have ended the matter, but the teenager decided to attack. Fingers shaped like claws on an animal, she reached through the open window and scratched my neck. I leaned away and held her at arm's length, she swinging and clawing. I would have clobbered her, but she was just a kid. I looked to her mother to restrain the girl, but she seemed to enjoy her out-of-control daughter.

Finally, she said, "Come on, Suzie, leave the bitch alone. Let's get out of here."

Dazed, I locked the car and hurried into the auditorium.

Fluff asked, "What happened to you?"

I felt a sting when I touched the wound and my fingers were stained with blood. I began to pour out an explanation in a single breath, but Fluff lost interest before I could state my concern.

"Grab some tissues and get in line on stage."

Lesson learned: When everyday stings set me back, I get up on the stage of life, sing and dance until the pain goes away. The hurt when Mom passes will need more healing than any memoir.

Over the years, my friends and I have tried to define just what showgirls are, most recently exchanging our views on social media. When in that role, we never perform bawdy or vulgar dance moves. Save that for burlesque and strip shows, and who knows what goes on in the privacy of escort services? Our stride requires a walking technique called "tipping" in which the motion is so smooth that exposed breasts do not bounce or jiggle. The most private area of the female body is covered with a g-string, and concealed by her *cooch* stance, thighs crossed at the crotch. A spread-leg position has no place on stage, however, long legs is an asset. All this in high heels with forty-pound headdresses and elaborate concoctions strapped to our backs.

Showgirls embody and celebrate exquisite feminine beauty. Our features are enhanced with long, thick false eyelashes, bright red lipstick, fishnet stockings, high heels, and excellent posture. Stylized poses and choreography on stage maximize our curvaceous, female bodies. When in character, we are defined by the extravagance and glitz of Bob Mackie's original costumes decked out in jewelry and by Donn Arden's creative productions.

And, what better location than the *Ziegfeld* stage at Bally's to accent ostrich-feathered, face-rouged, and high-heeled showgirl mystique than descending glittery stairs and astride platforms lowered from the ceiling over the heads of the audience. Or, a Biblical Delilah in showgirl costume dancing ballet-style with Sampson before he collapses the pillars and the roof caves in? Or, the most memorial technological device, sinking of the Titanic with thousands of gallons of water splashing on stage?

The image of a showgirl is a brand like *Coca Cola* or *Sara Lee*, and when in costume, each individual is responsible to maintain an established integrity both on and off stage. When hawkers use *showgirl* to peddle strippers and worse, it is an attack on what we represent. A personal experience, my showgirl image on the backs of bridge playing cards only to discover full naked bodies in lewd poses added after I signed the contract. I had to sue to get them off the market.

Showgirls can and often do integrate into the community to fulfill a social need. When HIV/AIDS hit the entertainment industry especially hard, we freely participated in many benefit performances. I spoke to dance classes long before I started one of my own.

Like athletes, showgirls have a limited career span, and many develop other saleable skills while still performing. Successful post-career showgirls include Maria Battagalia, whose agency *Always Entertaining* supplied a former mayor with abundant show-girls, and Tracy, distributor of Mary Kay products. The Metro Police Department employs Anthony Brown, of *Sampson and Delilah*, his wife, Dawn, the first black Bluebell to dance in *Jubilee*. My ex roommate, Katie, became an attorney and her friend a judge. I own Mikel's *Performing Arts Academy* and hold an Esthetician license in California and Nevada. Entertainers have families and second careers.

CHAPTER 17

Opportunities arise through networking and meeting people, activities as much fun as they are productive. You never know when a *Candid Camera* captures the moment, be it a performance or merely a friendly chat. My *Gemini* grabbed opportunities by their tails as they glided by, some I had little choice but to accept, like positive results of a pregnancy test. Caroline knew but I hadn't yet told Mom.

To take my mind off missing my second consecutive period, I went to hear Dennis Casey Parks, a former *Jubilee* singer, perform at Alexis Park Lounge. I approached him taking his break between sets.

"Hi." From the stare Dennis' girlfriend gave me, I felt a need to explain. "I just came from *Jubilee* to catch your late show." Her gaze continued to penetrate. Had I forgotten to take off my false eyelashes?

"Have a seat." Dennis half stood until he realized I had seated myself, his girlfriend unmoved.

"Thank you." I faced her. "You seem to recognize me."

"Mikel, this is one of my female vocalists, Barbara Blaire."

I knew who she was, but her up and down scrutiny felt uncomfortable. "Have we met? I feel you're trying to place me like from back in high school or something."

Barbara broke eye contact and faced Dennis. "Yeah, I agree. She's perfect."

"We better explain. Barbara and I caught your performance with Business Theater and liked what we saw. Seeing you up close, we're sure." They exchanged nods. "We're contracted to do a song and dance number for the '88 Pre-Olympics in Seoul Korea this summer."

Barbara said, "Dennis wants you and seven others who match your features to join our entourage."

Nineteen-hundred-and-eighty-eight not half-over and career changing event number two: probably pregnant and a chance at my second Olympics. I needed time to think, not whether to accept, but how a pregnancy would fit into the equation. However, first things first.

***

My body trembling, heart pounding, I held my breath. Ten seconds and still no *click* followed by a dial tone.

"Are you sure?" Jeff found his voice, and my self-confidence crept up a notch.

"Two out of three indications, missing my periods and a positive reading on a pregnancy test."

"And the third?" His voice almost a whisper.

"We have to wait seven more months for that level of proof."

Long pause but still no *click*. "What are you planning to do about it?"

"I didn't get pregnant by myself." *Breathe, breathe, breathe.*

"Are you sure it was me?"

All pent up air escaped my lungs in a burst. "No, one of the gay guys suddenly felt a heterosexual urge. Of course, it's your child." Child? As if pregnancy had been the single issue. Until that exact moment, I hadn't seriously considered that a human being was forming in my body. "Please don't hang up." *Do not run away* was what I meant.

"I won't." A snorting smile, his familiar reaction to the girls and gays teasing when Fluff was away. "This is more serious than my breaking your little toe."

Better yet, I had broken the ice. Jeff would stand by me, three years together in *Jubilee*, half that time as a couple, always kept secret because Fluff frowned on cast members fraternizing. *Easter Bunny*, his name for me from when I volunteered to distribute Easter eggs in costume to needy children. A powerful dancer featured in *Dance Magazine*; Christian, funny, intelligent, ideal genes to produce a beautiful child too soon in my career.

"Will you return so we can decide what to do?"

"Does Fluff know?"

"Not yet. I've only told my sister so far. Please come back, if just for a few hours."

"What good would that do?"

"You're my dance partner."

"Yeah, one dance too many."

"Not our only dance back in our apartment, just the one that really mattered."

"Why weren't you taking precautions?" I refused to respond, and he didn't push. He knew his responsibility. We had discussed his options. I couldn't chance gaining weight by taking the pill.

"Give me a few weeks to close on a couple of real estate sales, and we can talk."

After an uncomfortable pause, we spoke over each other, and I gave way. "You go first…"

More silence, and then the bombshell, "I'm sending you some money in case you decide to—"

"Don't you dare!" I hung up and finished my conversation into a dead phone. "If you walk out on me now, watching the Olympics on TV will be the only time you will ever see me, and you'll never get to know your son." I felt sure my baby would be a boy and, his name will not be *Jeffrey Jr.*

We wasted two postage stamps, Jeff sending me a check and my returning it.

***

"Mikel, to my office ASAP," Fluff's voice over the P.A. heard by all in the dressing room after the late show. Wardrobe had just removed my finale costume, and I stared into the mirror at the pooching around my lower abdomen. I knew why Fluff wanted to see me.

"Mikel, you are gaining weight." The greeting I dreaded but expected.

"I'm pregnant." From her expression, I might have announced that I had leprosy.

"Had you planned this?"

"It just happened."

"Has the guy—might not I just say, Jeff—agreed to take care of this problem?" Fluff never missed a thing with her people.

"He's into denial."

"Well, I'm sure Jeff will step up to the plate."

Tears formed. I needed to get out of her office.

"I hope you realize this is not a good situation. Had you come to see me, we could have talked it through." She glanced down at her desk and then up at the clock on the wall. "Settle this with Jeff and get back to me."

When I returned to my apartment, I stood naked in front of my full-length bedroom mirror and studied my midsection.

Jeffrey Gysin, now take a good look at your *Easter Bunny*. I laughed through tears, got angry, and then thought of Mom. She raised two daughters on her own. That's not the life I wanted. I dried my eyes and made up my mind. God allowed me this opportunity, and if I reject His gift, He might never offer it again. And if Jeff won't cooperate....

I awoke fresh and comfortable with my decision, even considered the bright side. Having a baby would be an acceptable excuse to leave *Jubilee* temporarily, although very few girls chose that course. Quitting without proper notice to participate in the Olympics would get me blackballed for any future dance jobs in Vegas, certainly no chance Fluff would take me back. Nicholas, already named by my Mom, saved the day. I took a deep breath, picked up the phone, and made the call to inform Jeff that I decided to keep the baby with or without him.

After sensing Fluff's eyes all over me during two shows that evening, I stopped by Alexis Park Lounge to give Dennis and Barbara my answer. Jeff had agreed to return to Vegas in a few days and discuss our situation. He and Fluff will have to accept my decision.

Dennis and Barbara were quietly having drinks at a table where I joined them. "I accept the offer to dance for you in the Olympics."

Dennis asked, "Fluff gave you the time off, almost two weeks counting travel time?"

"We worked it out." I attempted to keep my pregnancy a secret even from Dennis and Barbara, certainly the Olympic Committee had to be left in the dark. Caroline worked the numbers, four-and-a-half months pregnant by mid May, the approximate dates I would be dancing in Seoul, Korea.

Dennis pushed his drink aside. "Here's the scoop. We will audition for seven more dancers immediately."

"I'm the only one so far?"

"Matching your face and body will be our first criteria for selecting the others and by how well they follow your moves. Clear your calendar for the next few weeks of afternoon rehearsals. We are on a tight schedule."

"I'll be available evenings, too."

"Fluff fired you!" He shook his head. "Are you sure this is worth losing a career?"

"Actually, I'm a little bit pregnant, and she guessed almost immediately." For me, hiding any truth required constant vigilance, not something inherent in my personality. I needed a co-conspirator in this deception. "I'm sure she won't keep me on much longer." All my cards spread on the table, I trusted my friend's discretion.

"Are you up for this?" Barbara asked.

"I can get a written statement of approval from my gynecologist."

Dennis frowned and I panicked. "I don't need to know about your condition, the Olympic Committee certainly doesn't need to find out, and we better keep a low profile so Fluff won't discover what we are doing until its over."

I breathed a sigh of relief. "Thank you, Dennis."

"Kathy Lamar will join Barbara as back-up. You'll get to meet her when rehearsals start. In the mean time, Barbara will schedule auditions with the candidates we've prescreened. Blair Farrington is our choreographer, and Mort Stevens, the composer for *Hawaii Five-O*, will orchestrate."

***

Blair Farrington and Mort Stevens! It cannot get much better.

Dennis glanced toward the stage. "We need to get back up there. Any questions?"

"What about our costumes?"

"Las Vegas Showgirl, nothing less." Barbara stood and tugged on his arm.

"Does the group have a name?"

Dennis took a step toward the stage and turned. Walking backward, he waved his arm as if presenting something spectacular. "Recently back from the '88 Olympics, Dennis Casey Parks and Barbara Blaire with *The Las Vegas Diamond Dancers*."

***

"Well?" Fluff stood waiting for me in the dressing room between shows. Caught in the spotlight, I was not able to describe Jeff's and my encounter earlier that day, intense and even intimate in a strange sort of way. By returning his check, he understood my decision before I made it clear over the phone. He flew back so we could talk face-to-face. We chose our favorite quiet spot at Willow Beach on Lake Mead to discuss my pregnancy. Opposing armies had negotiated truces on terms that were more comfortable.

I grant for you and you alone, words that terminated our relationship and freed me of any guilt for not sharing my son with his father or his father's family. His offering money for an abortion made me angry, but my spirit soared. I made the right decision.

I faced Fluff. "I'm raising my baby without Jeff." I ignored the curious stares of the dancers.

"Are you sure you can handle this by yourself?"

"Yes."

She nodded, not in agreement but an *it's your life* gesture. "Stop by the personnel office tomorrow morning to sign for your leave of absence and receive your final paycheck." Starting tomorrow, Diane will fill in until further notice."

I gave Fluff the benefit of the doubt for her immediate decision. A pregnant showgirl could create a liability for the company.

I was granted a year's medical coverage but, for obvious reasons according to management, no job guarantee afterwards. I felt sure I could work my body back into shape, and my performance over the past three and a half years should be worth something.

I had the '88 Pre-Olympics to concentrate on and then prepare a *nest* for the baby developing in my body.

CHAPTER 18

We practiced Blair Farrington's dance sequence at his studio, knowing we would have only one full-compliment rehearsal at the Olympic Stadium in Korea.

Feeling comfortable with our routine, we packed up, boarded a Boeing 747 filled to capacity, our group of about a dozen clustered in the business section. Settling in for an eleven-hour flight, I had difficulty sleeping in a seat that only reclined slightly. Landing at Seoul's Incheon International Airport, Bob Hope, Brooke Shields, Jermaine Jackson, Julio Iglesias, Loretta Swit, and Rich Little exited the VIP section of the plane, waving to the crowd as they walked the red carpet to a string of black limousines. We followed down that same carpet to regular sized Hyundai Excels, also black.

Dad, if you could see your daughter ride in a foreign-made car now. My black Camaro with *SHOWGRL* license plates—sorry *BARYSH*, you'd been jilted—would have been a more impressive ride to our hotel.

The morning before the opening ceremonies, we were shuttled to the Olympic Park and gathered around the massive granite sculpture in front of the new Olympic Stadium, all built for the upcoming event. *Dennis Casey Parks and The Las Vegas Diamond*

Dancers rehearsed in front of an audience of mostly American celebrities waiting their turn on stage.

Brooke Shields wandered over to visit after I finished my stretch exercises. Two years younger than me, she was working her way through college by performing with Bob Hope. We shared our unique acting experiences, she as an actress going nude in *Blue Lagoon*, and I as a topless *Jubilee* Showgirl; her mentor, Bob Hope, and mine, Gene Nelson.

Waiting our turn to perform, I surveyed the cheering crowd of eighty thousand spectators, mostly Koreans and an occasional group of American soldiers. Chills up and down my spine, as thirteen thousand Korean performers down on the arena grounds marched to the rhythm of a thousand percussion instruments.

Brooke Shields and Bob Hope sang a duet and did a comedy routine introducing *Hodori*, the official smiling tiger mascot for the '88 Olympics. The Korean tiger reminded me of Kellogg's Corn Flakes Mom used to give Caroline and me for breakfast. I half-expected Tony-the-Tiger to shout, "They're grrreat."

Dennis Casey Parks and The Las Vegas Diamond Dancers performed flawlessly, and we earned a loud but polite response from the crowd, nothing like "Buffalo Gals Won't You Come Out Tonight" or "Rhapsody in Blue" at Los Angeles.

I was jazzed. Four years since the '84 Olympics and a lifetime of events in between.

Our cluster of American performers mingled together as a family, traveling, entertaining, sight seeing, and, of course, taking and signing pictures. We walked around the city and shopped. The Korean shopkeepers were very polite. In their culture, it was considered rude to answer 'no' to our questions. They would say 'yes, yes' but only meant *I understand your question*, not necessarily agreeing on price. This led to several misunderstandings when negotiating.

I bought my family leather jackets, wallets, and jewelry. I found a pair of Nikki baby shoes for my son, Nicholas Bryce. By then, Mom and Caroline had decided both my baby's names. *Peterson* would be my contribution.

I kept a flat abdomen, the hardest part eating Korean food. My stomach could not stand even the smell of ginseng, a cabbage and garlic dish. I managed to keep my secret from everyone except Dennis and Barbara, who totally ignored the issue. Had anyone found out, I would have been barred from the performance.

Our flight back to Vegas, we resembled a plane-load of exhausted tourists leaving Sin City, emotionally spent but exhilarated and ready to resume routine lives.

Nineteen hundred and eighty eight will stick in my memory as the year I came down with a terminal case of maturity that would frighten and delight me the rest of my life. It didn't set in overnight like the common cold. It gnawed away my innocence since I left Albuquerque, rode the waves between successes and crises, each cycle gaining momentum and intensity until presto, maturity! Just in time for the mother of all nail-biters, giving birth. On the way to this end-of-the-year miracle, I experienced a major career shift and a somewhat shaky new relationship back in California, climaxed with nine pounds of all-boy popping out of my body and into my chaotic life.

Arriving back from Korea, Dennis handed the members of his Olympic team a handwritten invitation to a welcome-home party in his back yard, in parentheses, *Come day or night, whenever your work schedule allows.* I had no day job or night job. Any temporary employment would cancel my leave of absence from *Jubilee* and Business Theater, including medical benefits.

As my overstuffed suitcase tumbled out of the chute and onto the carrousel, a tinge of loneliness swept over me. Duffle bag strapped over my shoulder and luggage wheels scratching across the sidewalk, I approached a cab, trunk lid up and rear door open.

"Where to?" The driver hoisted the larger piece into the back, but I clung to the duffle as if it contained the last of my possessions on earth.

"My apartment."

"Okay?" He closed my door and slid behind the wheel. "And that happens to be where?"

My mind foggy, his question didn't register. "What?"

The smile in the rear view mirror morphed into a scowl. "Where are we going?"

Rather than my current apartment, I rattled off the address of my studio apartment on Maryland Parkway. When the driver turned the wrong way out of the airport, I realized my mistake and made the correction. The cab crossed two lanes of traffic and made a u-turn, my duffle pinning me against the door.

I had been thinking about Willie, my former neighbor, probably why I gave the cabbie a wrong address. Willie was gone, I reminded myself, wishing to deny the fact. If he were still alive, I'd have skipped my apartment and headed to his place.

I missed my roommates, Rachael and her husband, Eric, and I briefly questioned my decision to live alone after Jeff left. I missed coming home to Tyler Murray and Camila Griggs in Van Nuys or to my cousin Venita and her family when I arrived in Vegas. Those people felt like home, some actually relatives.

I unloaded my luggage and sorted through clothes and Olympic mementos. Organizing gifts for friends and family spread across my bed revived my spirits.

I called Mom to tell her I got back safe, expecting to hear questions about my experience at the Pre-Olympics or, more likely, concerning my pregnancy. We had only one serious talk about my condition, our second phone conversation after breaking the news, our first little chat cut short. I hadn't yet mentioned that

Caroline Elizabeth Peterson

Michelle Jeanne Peterson

"We're dressed and ready for church, Texas Papa"

Sandia High School Albuquerque, New Mexico

Senior year varsity cheerleading

High school modern dance team

Mikel received a
scholarship with
Jaime Rogers at
Debbie Reynolds
Studio in 1982

295

GILL

Dolphins, Saints
plan scrimmage
SPORTS, 3C

Rock audiences sold
on Melle Mel's rap
LIVING TODAY, 1D

Mostly
Sunny
Details on 2A

The Miami Herald

Saturday, July 28, 1984

Five years in the making,
Olympics will open tonight

JOE STARITA
Herald Staff Writer

LOS ANGELES - After five years and $500 million, after mega-dollops of hype and hoopla and a 9,000-mile torch run, through heat and smog, boycotts and big business, all is ready.

At 7:30 this evening, the Hollywood Olympics will unfold in America's living rooms on a scale that threatens to make Cecil B. DeMille seem like a two-bit stagehand in a B-grade talkie.

Armed with the most dazzling electronics in their Star Wars arsenal, the Los Angeles Summer Games will offer a 3½-hour opening to plan and is expected to be seen by 2.5 billion people — more than half the world's population.

Olympic community will see is a thundering flashdance ensemble of all-out Americana, a $7-million, Yankee-style blowout brought to life on the 4½-acre floor of the Los Angeles Coliseum by a cast of 18,000.

Top billing for tonight's world premiere goes to Ronald Reagan, an old cowhand who knows something about California, lavish productions and the inner machinations of Hollywood. In keeping with Olympic tradition, President Reagan — as the head of state for the host nation — will formally open the Games of the 23rd Olympiad. Before leaving on a

L.A.'84

The race for souls / 20A

A heavyweight's
journey / 1C

DAVID TURNLEY / Knight-Ridder Olympics
Mikel Peterson rehearses for the Olympics opening

1984 Olympics Ceremonies in Las Angeles, California

"With your talent and long legs, Vegas offers you the best career opportunities."

Gene Nelson
actor/director/producer

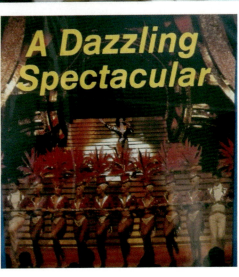

A Dazzling Spectacular

City Lites at the Flamingo Hilton Hotel and Casino 1984

Mikel in
Jubilee at the
MGM Grand
Hotel
1984 to 1988

Sammy
Davis Jr.

Jerry Lewis

Mikel meet and greet
Celebrebrities in
MGM Celebrity Room

"How is it going, Baby?"

Dean Martin

"Just great, Dean!"

MGM/Bally's Hotel Business Theatre 1984 - 1992

"Give us that blond dancer
with the exuberant smile!"

Joe Morris
Business Theatre
Director

Jubilee 4 1/2 Months Pregnant

Dean Martin

Sylvestor Stallone

Sammy Davis Jr.

Mikel has cherished
memories of celebrity
encounters as a
Jubilee showgirl

Wayne Newton

Jerry Lewis

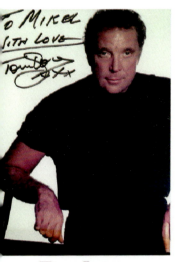

Tom Jones

Righteous
Brothers

Robert Wagner

Sam Kinison

Mel Tellis

Kenny Rogers

**Brook Shield and
Blair Farrington**

1988 Olympics in Seoul, Korea

**Loretta Swit
Julio Iglasias**

To Mike,
I met your
mom. Sorry it was
such a short visit.
Love,
Brooke xx

Brook Shields

Jermaine Jackson

Bob Hope

Rich Little

LA CAGE

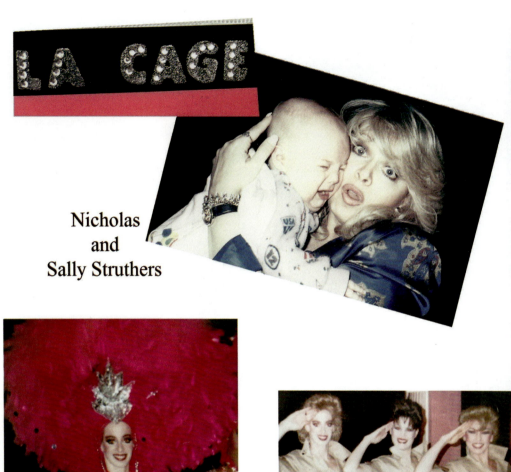

Nicholas
and
Sally Struthers

Los Angeles LaCage Impersonators Show 1988 - 1989

"SHOW OF THE YEAR"

RIVIERA
Hotel & C
Las Veg

MAY 12-18, 1989 – ENTERTAINMEN

MOTOR
BOAT
SHOW

THUNDERBIRDS VISIT "SPLASH" — Air Force Thunderbird pilots were welcomed backstage recently by
Kutash's "Splash" at the Riviera Hotel & Casino. The pilots, whose high-speed precision maneuvers in their
Falcons drew large crowds at Nellis Air Force Base last week, were accompanied by the official Navy aero-
tion team, The Blue Angels (not shown). The "Angels," based at Pensacola Naval Air Station in Florida,
from one show site to another when they decided to visit their counterparts in Las Vegas.

SPLASH

Mikel in *Splash* at the
Riviera Hotel and Casino
1989

MGM Grand
Business Theatre

Nicholas and Mommy

Nick B. Peterson
Hair: Brown / Eyes: Hazel
Date of Birth: 10-23-88

My Son Nicholas

Muhammed Ali

Buddy Ebsen

Claude Van Damme

Robert Goulet

Mikel as Susan Anton

Post Card Girl Souvenirs

Siegfried and
Nicholas

Mikel in *Siegfried and Roy*
at the Mirage Hotel and Casino
1990 - 1992

Siegfried

Elizabeth
Taylor

Michael Jackson

Siegfried and Roy
Mikel Controls the
movement of seven puppet
soldiers on stage

André Duran
Meiers

Hair: Sandy Blond / Eyes: Hazel
Date of Birth: 9-13-98

My Son Andre'

Brooke Sheilds

Melinda Lady of Magic

Dolph Lundgren

Dolly Parton

Amilio Estevez

Steven Spielberg

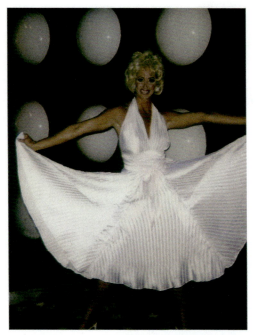

Mikel as Marilyn Monroe

Joan Collins

Sam Kinison

Mikel as Liza Minnelli

Mikel meets Liza Minnelli

Mikel in *Caboret Cirus* at the
Lady Luck Hotel and Casino 1992

Mikel and James Brown
Mars Attack

Mikel in *Wild Thing* at the Dunes Hotel 1992

WILD THINGS

y Berosini & Kirby VanB
by Breck Wall & Patrick Maes • Choreographed by Michael
Now Appearing in the Persian Room

Mikel danced in the
Dunes Hotel and Casino
Wild Thing Show
1992

Mikel's pride and joy, her boys
Nick and Andre´

Suzanne Peterson
Sue Peterson
Gary Peterson
Candace Peterson
Mikel Peterson
Caroline Peterson
Nicholas Peterson

Alaska

Nicholas Peterson
Mikel Peterson
Caroline Peterson
Candace Peterson

Hawaii

Suzanne Peterson
Andre Meiers
Scott Meiers
Nicholas Peterson
Mikel Peterson
Caroline Peterson
Candace Peterson

Seattle

Grandpa and
Grandma House

San Felipe de Neri

Mikel's Mom and Dad

Old Town New Mexico

♡ My mom ♡

Dad, Debbie, Caroline,
Mikel, and Mom

Mom on stage with Matt Goss

Mikel performs at fifty
years old in
Sassy: Showgirl Follies

Stasha and Nick

Andre' and Grandma

Don King

Mike Tyson

Caesar Chavez

Leon Spinks

First inaugural Las Vegas boxing Hall of Fame
Hall of Fame Sportswriter, Royce Feour

Jeff abandoned me. She would tell me to come home to have the baby, but that would be admitting defeat.

Neither issue had been her concern. "Did you go to church while you were there?"

Back home in Albuquerque, our family attended Church-of-Christ services Sundays and Wednesdays. As children, she dressed Caroline and me in our Sunday best and sent Texas Papa pictures as proof that the Catholic fathers of Betty Jeanne's girls did not contaminate their Barker Church-of-Christ heritage. We attended Catholic services when visiting Grandpa Lesmen, especially Midnight Mass on Christmas Eve. I went to church twice a week in California, here in Vegas only on the Lord's Day.

Caroline and I often discussed our conflicted life styles with Texas Papa's religion, she being gay and I never married to the man I happened to be living with. I hadn't felt guilty about any gap in my faith until Mom's question. I made some excuse about not having church access in Seoul, but our conversation started me thinking.

Everything had me thinking: my go-it-alone pregnancy and the loss of Business Theater and *Jubilee*—hopefully temporary—following a high point in my career. What was the foundation from which I approached the challenges confronting me? Go to bed expecting to wake up with plan "B" in hand? Until then, I always had a backup.

My brain zeroed in on Mom's question and would not let up. Going to church had been my family's tradition, and it felt good. However, I believed fate determined life's options, and self interest guided my choices.

A flash of my mother's situation hit me like a ton of bricks. It scared the wits out of me. Am I on the way to becoming Betty Jeanne Peterson, an accomplished woman who dropped her career to dedicate her herself to her two youngest children? I love you,

Mom, but I do not want to end up like you. Please admit that you love Jim Mesnard and wrap your arms around your wonderful friend and tell him you need him in your life day and night. It will make all of us more comfortable.

My father wanted to please Mom, but he got tired and left. I forgave him, perhaps Mom hadn't. He allowed me the freedom to test my wings, but Mom still hovered over me. My life style, so different from Caroline's, matched my father's more than my mother's.

Throughout my career, I felt comfortable with older men, even my nosey neighbor back in Van Nuys, certainly Willie in Las Vegas. Three decades later, my friends, Don and Cliff, hang around while I teach water aerobics to other seniors. I'm a caregiver in my home to a retired Viet Nam General.

***

At Dennis' first all-night party to celebrate our Olympic success, a familiar voice came from behind me. "And you, young lady, wouldn't dance topless for us in *Moulin Rouge*." I turned to face Walter Cartier, laughing and reaching out to greet me. His good humor was contagious.

"But who will pay to see a mother strutting her stuff?" I joked.

"Once a showgirl, always a showgirl. You'll still be strutting your stuff when you're my age."

Fifty years old, I guessed, and how right he was. "Picture showgirl-me with a baby in my arms."

"All the more intriguing." He busted out laughing, then became serious. "Had you accepted my offer, *Moulin Rouge* might have overtaken *Jubilee* as number one in Vegas."

We became good friends, not missing any of the Pre-Olympic troupe's annual celebrations for years to come. I considered Walter and Dennis as my celebrity mentors along with Gene Nelson and Buddy Ebsen, and counting. My intimate relationships up to that point, Stephen, Douglas, Michael, and Jeff, on the way to a dozen before my final showgirl performance. Who knows what my future holds?

Dennis and Barbara hosted my baby shower and invited many of the dancers who brought diapers, baby accessories, and an update of life at *Jubilee* without Mikel. My girlfriend, Paige, told me that the nudes are talking about having babies. If Mikel can do it on her own, why can't we who have husbands? I didn't admit that raising my son as a single mom wasn't my first choice.

She suggested, "You need to get out during night hours when you earned your living. You can't just sit around waiting for the baby to come."

I exercised during the day when not sleeping and went clubbing around with friends at night. I loved being pregnant after the nausea went away, but why did God make it take so long to have a baby? From when I arrived in Vegas up until my role in *Jubilee* took less time.

At the Shark Club one evening, a gorgeous Italian man stepped up and introduced himself, Vince Primerano, from Syracuse, New York, and offered to buy me a cocktail. I ordered a virgin strawberry daiquiri. He probably noticed my condition, but I felt no need to explain why the non-alcoholic drink. When not pregnant, I drank regular cocktails but maintained control by limiting myself to one or two drinks, nursing them all night. I credited my Gemini for creating this moment.

Vince grinned. "What does a nice girl like you do in a town like this?"

I caught the not-so-subtle implication. "Your guess is way off the mark. I'm not even a stripper." Time to titillate. "However, I do go topless in public."

"You're a dancer?"

"A *Jubilee* Showgirl. On temporary leave." He could decide why I'm not working. To change the subject, I could have mentioned that his cologne intoxicated me, but that would have given away too much of how I felt. "What brings you to Las Vegas?"

"I run a business in California and needed to take a break."

A wave of memories of a time and place swept over me, as if my two years' experience in California had replaced Albuquerque as home. "I went to Debbie Reynold's Dance Studio in Hollywood," two names anyone would recognize. "Was an extra in a couple of movies."

"I seldom get up that way, but it sounds intriguing. Maybe you could show me around the next time you get back there."

No time like the present. "I haven't been there in four years, and I miss the place." Actually, only Gene Nelson, Tyler, and Camila.

"Well that settles it." He handed me his business card. "Let me know when you're coming."

Was that it, *see you around*?

He gulped his drink. "Now, you are going to show me the hot spots in this city."

After a couple of nightclubs and a sunrise over Lake Mead, he proved to be a gentleman by not making any sexual advances. Before kissing me goodnight at my doorstep, he said, "With your permission, I'd like to buy you a round trip airline ticket to visit me in Huntington Beach. You get to choose the days that are most convenient for you."

I needed to see this man on his home turf. "Thank you. I'll check with my step-sister in Van Nuys to see when she is available for me to stay overnight."

"I'd love to meet her, but you'll be staying in Huntington Beach. A motel if you turn down the hospitality of my town home." He smiled. "It has two bedrooms."

The dates confirmed, my tickets arrived, and I spent three days at his home. In his kitchen over coffee, he asked, "Something troubling you?"

Was this the moment?

"Would you like to talk about it?"

My gaze moved from the tiled floor up to his eyes. "I'm pregnant."

"A party girl drinking a virgin daiquiri, you were quite obvious."

"I never tried to hide it."

"Nothing changes what has developed between us. Just adds another dimension to our relationship. I like you and let's see where this goes. You never can tell until you test the water."

We didn't just test the water but dove right in. I sub-leased my apartment, put my furniture in storage, and loaded my Camaro as I had done with *Barysh* six years earlier in Albuquerque. Vince and I became a couple, soon to be a family.

My pregnancy leave covered eighty percent of my medical costs, and I used some of my savings to pay the difference and to take cosmetology classes as an esthetician. I did not want nursing as a second career like Mom, but I needed a backup in case anything happened that I couldn't perform. I was a single mom without help from my son's father.

I kept busy with classes, exercising, and eating a proper diet. I amazed Vince with my cooking skills. I graduated shortly before my due date, but held off getting a job at a beauty shop.

Vince stood by me throughout my pregnancy, but he would show me pictures from his *Playboy Magazine*. That hurt, especially knowing I had turned down an offer from a *Playboy* scout to be featured in an article as a showgirl. He expressed an unusually friendly interest in one of my Esthetician classmates, wondering what it would be like to have her stay overnight.

I made sure Vince never felt deprived sexually, and he responded favorably, except for those few off-handed remarks. He shouldn't have teased, because showgirls are very meticulous about how they look and feel. The most perfectly shaped body on stage cannot hide an inner feeling of ugly or even small imperfections. We are a touchy group of performers.

CHAPTER 20

"This baby is ready to come. If nothing happens between now and Friday, we're going to induce labor."

I phoned Caroline immediately for her opinion—she agreed—and we flew Mom to California right away rather than wait for Nicholas to arrive.

Early Friday morning, Vince drove Mom and me to the hospital where they administered an epidural. I sat around for six hours before they punctured the membrane. It felt like a water balloon popped between my legs.

I didn't experience any discomfort. My sister Caroline checked all procedures and assured me everything had been done according to *Hoyle*, or whoever was the patron saint of baby doctors. Mother, being a nurse as well as giving birth to six children, was surprised at the change in procedures since her time. She approved numbing the pain, but husbands, unless they were medical men like Dr. Peterson, should not be in the delivery room.

When I asked Vince to take pictures of the birth process, she gasped, "I supposed this is the new way to bring babies into the world."

Funny what I recall from those final minutes before Nicholas demanded all my attention; the concerned expression on Vince's face and Mom's feet pacing back and forth visible under the curtain. She was nervous because it was my first. What bothered me was going through the delivery without my sister at my side. I laughed to think she might be delivering another woman's baby at that exact time.

"One more big push." I saw the doctor but heard my sister's voice.

Vince's free hand tightened its grip, as he raised the camera. Through my view in the mirror, out squeezed the top of a head. I couldn't wait. The instincts of my body and my natural determination since childhood gave that final push.

"It's a boy." A chorus of voices.

"What a cute baby," the nurse said as she walked away with him.

With my feet in stirrups and the doctor messing with me, I yelled, "Vince, follow her and see that she doesn't get my baby mixed up with another one."

The doctor chuckled, and I considered breaking my legs loose and squeezing his head in a scissor hold. The nurse returned and laid Nicholas on my chest.

My body shook and I cried for joy from the wonderful gift God had given me. It amazed me how God's world worked, how awesome is the human body.

Vince counted the baby's fingers and toes. At that moment, Nicholas became his child. The hard part happened when my boobs blew up to the size of Dolly Parton's. I yelled, "Hurry and get that breast pump."

Nicholas declared healthy, I rejoiced, *thank you God*. Mom called Caroline and described Nicholas as *those funny nine-and-a-half pounds*.

I brought my baby home slightly under his birth weight, but the nurse assured me this was normal. The pressure and pain in my breasts had been excruciating, but soon a balance developed between Nicholas' hunger and my milk supply. All seemed to go well until he started losing weight after a couple of months.

The doctor said, "Sometimes women with active lives choose to stop breast feeding. This is natural." His gaze settled on the clipboard. "Anxiety and even mild depression following the trauma of giving birth can disrupt the milk flow."

I hadn't experienced postpartum, but I was eager to start dancing again. Mom, my ready-made babysitter, flew back to Albuquerque after we celebrated Christmas together. Vince arranged to make some of his sales calls from home, and I hit the road searching for dance jobs. When Nicholas switched from breast milk to Isomil, I expanded my job-search area. A position with a group of three female dancers with one female impersonator opened at *La Cage Theater* in West Hollywood. I auditioned and was accepted. My self-esteem zoomed.

I drove forty-five miles to West Hollywood and danced one performance a night six times a week. The job was worth the Los Angeles freeway commute. Vince fed and played with Nicholas before putting him down for the night, and I had all day to pamper my baby.

LaCage Aux Folles had a decade-long tradition of men impersonating entertainers such as Diana Ross, Marilyn Monroe, Cher, Bette Midler, Tina Turner, and others. It operated in a building independent of any restaurant or casino, quite different from theaters in Las Vegas. Details of dress, make up, and mannerism were imitated so precisely, that it was nearly impossible to tell they were not the actual person. Lip-syncing their recorded voices added to the illusion. Only one of the actors sang with his own voice in falsetto.

Our costumes included flamboyant showgirl headgear as well as bugle-boy uniforms from the forty's. I missed the *Jubilee* production with jeweled-and-feathered dancers descending the central staircase and epic scenes of temple pillars ripped away and the Titanic sinking. Men in drag replaced tuxedoed men with rhinestone vests. At *Jubilee*, the gay guys liked to dress up and dance as showgirls when Fluff wasn't around. The female impersonators were not all gay, but they enjoyed dressing and acting as females.

Our cast became a family—more informal than *Jubilee*—and we played to a different kind of audience. Without having to follow a strict formula, we were allowed to improvise. A natural break from character would bring down the house.

The male dancer in showgirl costume joined our routines, and we dressed frumpy to accompany his Aretha Franklin impersonation. One male-to-male impersonator lip-synced Prince's "Purple Rain."

Vince brought Nicholas the night Sally Struthers came to our performance. The cast, male and female, took turns playing with my son when not on stage. Sally posed for a picture with Nicholas in her arms, and he fussed. At nine months old, he had not yet learned to show his better side in front of the camera. His attitude would change.

Dad and Judy came to watch me perform and to meet Nicholas, his only grandchild shared with my mom. I just knew Dad and Vince would hit it off, because they were so much alike. Maybe that was why Mom and Vince never saw things eye-to-eye. Unfortunately, Mom didn't make it out to see my show.

Paige and Washington stayed overnight in our second bedroom and, so she claimed later, went home pregnant. I felt for sure Fluff would blame me for encouraging Paige.

Couples often stay together for the sake of their children, and I think that was somewhat Vince's and my situation. I attributed part of our growing apart to my being lonesome for my old friends in Vegas.

Feeding Nicholas one morning, I blurted, "Nicholas and I are moving back to Vegas." I glanced across the table at Vince. "You can go with us or stay here."

Vince faked a shocked expression. He knew it was bound to happen, and he made a quick decision. "I'll go with you guys. As a company rep, I can develop a clientele back there as well as here in California."

I wasn't sure which of his two choices I would have preferred. My trust in his fidelity began to erode back when I was pregnant and he flaunted his *Playboy* centerfold in my face. My friend from back at esthetician school, hardly a *bunny* type from his magazine, roused his interest in a *menage a trios.* I disregarded the idea as his idle fantasy, annoying but he would lose interest when I was no longer pregnant. My growing mid section never interfered with our intimacy or my exercise routine, my usual workout followed by a three-and-a-half mile run each morning.

I regained my shape quickly, but Vince still had a threesome stuck in the back of his mind. After a day on the beach with my friend, we came back to my place sweaty and thirsty.

Vince brought us cocktails and said, "I hope you gals didn't sunbathe topless and create a scandal."

I should never have told him that *Jubilee* Showgirls partied bare breasted down on Lake Mead to avoid an uneven tan.

"My tan lines aren't noticeable at *LaCage.*" I sipped my drink and faced my friend. "Bring me up to date. Do beauticians work topless these days?"

"Maybe under our smocks." She giggled. "When the right guy comes in, we flash him." She flung her Kimono beach robe open as far as the cinched belt around her waist.

Her modest two-piece swimsuit didn't deter Vince's imagination. He caught my attention and gestured with his head toward our guest. I knew what he wanted but ignored the hint.

When she went to the bathroom, he pleaded. "Ask her. I think she'll do it if you make the suggestion."

A threesome was not something I found intriguing, but, after our girl-talk that afternoon, I felt quite sure she would like the naughty aspect of it.

"Please."

She walked in on our whispering and asked, "What am I missing?"

I couldn't make up something on the spur of the moment that she wouldn't believe anyhow. "Vince would like to watch you and me make out."

She blushed but didn't gasp. "Like how?"

"Take off your tops," Vince suggested.

She glanced at me still in my two-piece.

"At least ditch the robe." Vince spread his hands in an open-up gesture.

She unknotted the belt and let both ends dangle from the loops. She slid one arm through its sleeve and then the other, all the while her eyes focused on me, like seeking permission.

"The bra." Vince's tone less demanding.

I nodded and we each reached behind and unfastened the snaps, she crossing her arms over her breasts, I letting it all hang out. Topless to me was not that big of a thing, but she remained cautious. I walked up to her and eased her arms to her side, "Are you sure you are okay with this?"

She nodded, raised one hand to my breast and then the other. The soft feminine touch wasn't anything new to me; male dancers' hands don't have calluses. She reached for my hand and covered her breast, a sensation I had not felt before. She kissed me with parted lips and wrapped her arms around me. For sure, that sensation was new, but weird.

I broke off the kiss and scanned the living room for a location more comfortable than standing in the kitchen being gawked at. My eye settled on the rocking chair Vince bought for me when I was nursing Nicholas. My mind's eye saw Mom there, gently rocking, neither approving nor disapproving of what her daughter was doing with this woman.

"I'm sorry. I can't do this." I held my friend's hands. "We aren't meant to be lovers, and we don't have to act out any man's fantasy."

She nodded, picked up her bra and robe and headed toward the bathroom.

I faced Vince and said, "I'll freshen our drinks if you start the barbeque." Heading toward the kitchen, I turned and said, "We can talk about this later."

A month passed and we still hadn't discussed the elephant in the room.

We grew more distant as a couple, but Vince had become increasingly important to Nicholas. Trusting our relationship as a family, I gave notice at *LaCage*. Vince wrapped up the appointments on his calendar, and we leased an apartment on West Tropicana over the phone and through the mail. One U-Haul load and we landed in Vegas, temporarily jobless. I immediately set out to correct that situation.

CHAPTER 21

Vince laid Nicholas down for his nap and began unpacking, while I went to Fluff's office as pre-arranged by phone. My year's medical leave had expired months ago, but no deadline had been established for rehiring. I had toned my body through exercise and honed my skills at the *La Cage* in Hollywood. I knew all the *Jubilee* dance routines, and could step right in after a couple of rehearsals. Furthermore, I always got along with the cast and upper management.

Fluff met me outside her office. "Mikel, you just don't look up to par like you used to." She shook her head. "With that being said, we do not have a position for you in *Jubilee.*"

Stunned, I gasped, ready to put up an argument. Instinct told me to hold my tongue, and better judgment deterred me from going over Fluff's head. She wasn't one to change her mind, and management would certainly back her decision. I needed to gather my dignity, thank Fluff for all she did for me in the past, and express my desire to be considered at some future date. But, she had already walked off, leaving me standing in the dressing area.

"I'm sorry, Mikel," a voice from behind a stack of costumes awaiting repairs. "Come and sit." My favorite wardrobe lady moved her sewing box to the floor and patted the chair. "Tell me about Nicholas."

I sobbed. We hugged and she handed me a tissue. "Your friends talked about you and your son all the time, until one-by-one they got pregnant and left the show."

I dabbed my eyes. "That's why Fluff wouldn't take me back!"

She patted my arm. "Do you have pictures of him?"

***

"You didn't get rehired?" Vince read rejection on my face when I returned to our apartment. "Can't you file a complaint to someone higher up?"

I shook my head, not ready for advice from him. In his tone, I sensed *we should have stayed in California.*

"We've got furniture to bring in and unpacking to do." I kicked an empty box out of my way to the bedroom to change into jeans. In an opened suitcase and snuggled between our unpacked clothes, Nicholas lay sound asleep. My mood brightened. I lost *Jubilee*, but I had my precious son. Together we would take on every challenge Las Vegas has to offer, starting with Business Theater.

At his office the next day, Joe Morris greeted me with encouraging words. "You're back just in time to do the Ford Industrial Show."

"You know that production was my favorite." Had he been aware Fluff refused to take me back? "You probably heard I won't be with *Jubilee.*"

"That's a downright shame." A hint of surprise in his voice. "I hope you're still willing to do Business Theater. Most of my girls are from Fluff's entourage."

"I wouldn't be jealous of them, if that's what you are wondering."

"Of course not." He blushed. "You're not the type to carry a grudge."

"I'm not angry with Fluff, and definitely won't hold you responsible." Almost too good to be true. I'm eager for the job while Joe worried I wouldn't accept his offer.

"The Ford Industrial rep will be happy to hear you're back. Always asks for that blond with the big smile." He glanced down at the calendar on his desk. "I would like to have you and Vince come to dinner next week. And please bring Nicholas. Would Thursday work for you?"

"I'm sure it would." Joe knew Vince's and Nicholas' names without my telling him. He probably knew Fluff's decision before I did.

"My partner, Frank, will prepare a gourmet barbeque, but he can whip up a child's dish."

My relationship with Joe Morris picked up where it left off, as if the time gap hadn't taken place.

While rehearsing for Ford Industrial, I parked Nicholas' stroller between two chairs, food on his left and toys on his right within easy reach. Colored lights and a cacophony of sound kept him entertained. By the time I warmed Nicholas' bottle during break, the girls had rushed to him, taking turns feeding him grapes. Sorry Fluff. More of your girls will be having babies.

We performed on the *Ziegfeld* Stage early in the afternoon, and my friends from the *Jubilee* cast crowded backstage to offer support. From my peripheral, I could barely make out their faces in the unlighted sidelines, cheering me on.

After the show, I followed them down to the dressing room, not caring what Fluff thought. I didn't hang around. It was too painful. Fluff stayed in her office.

Dennis and Barbara gave us a couple of weeks to settle in before hosting their second of many annual '88 Pre-Olympic celebrations. Kathy Lamar, Dennis' other back-up singer, was on tour and unable to attend. Nicholas and I held the center of attention, and Vince, oozing with Italian charm, blended with the group quite well. He did feeding and diapering duty, allowing me the freedom to mingle with my friends. I was proud of him.

We celebrated Nicholas' first birthday in the park on a sunny October afternoon surrounded by mostly *Jubilee* dancers. Paige and Dawn with husbands, who like me, left *Jubilee* to have families, but unlike me, did not want to go back. I never gave up my dream of being a dancer/showgirl, and my dreams never let go of the notion. Mornings, I would wake up wanting to go back to sleep for the dance finale. Yet, I never regretted my decision to have children, just sorry that Fluff would not accept me back. My friends railed out against her as being cruel, but I didn't wallow in pity. The memory of her insulting me remained too vivid. Nicholas' and my future were at stake.

I explored every legitimate dance opportunity in Vegas, if topless, all the better. My breasts had changed but remained solid. I soon realized *Jubilee* might be one of the last topless showgirl reviews. After three decades, *Lido de Paris* at the Stardust had been dying of old age, about to be replaced with *Enter the Night*. Unfortunately, auditions to the new show stressed vocal talent—no lip-syncing like at LaCage—as well as showgirl stage experience. And trained animals.

I objected to showgirls sharing the stage with Bobby Berosini and his performing orangutans. It cheapened *Enter the Night*, to my notion. As an animal lover, I disapproved of displaying monkeys as silly creatures and showgirls alongside apes. White tigers, on the other hand, demanded the dignity they deserved.

Splash at the Riviera remained an option. When I first arrived at Las Vegas in 1984, Jeff Kutash held auditions for aquatic dancers in the first staged water and light show. I had imagined myself in a one-piece swimsuit—my naïve notion of nudity back then—swimming in a huge fluted champagne glass, air bubbles surfacing to simulate Champagne tickling my legs. Humorous visions, speared at the end of a giant swizzle stick like an olive in a martini or squirming with a harpoon through my mid section tickled my funny bone.

Jeff Kutash's intended exotic vision never left the drawing board. In its place, a nineteen thousand gallon glassed-in water tank, none-the-less a creative and artistic concept. I hadn't auditioned for the show's grand opening back then in favor of a better opportunity with *Jubilee*. Who knows? I could have been another Esther Williams by now if I had.

I wouldn't trade my *Jubilee* experience for anything, but I needed a job and *Splash* might provide the opportunity.

I secured a meeting with Jeff Kutash to convince him that I knew how to swim as well as dance, quite different from being up on skates for the first time auditioning for *City Lites*. I sat across from him watching his pencil make scratch-designs on his note pad.

Without taking his eyes off the paper, he said, "I decided to take you on as a dancer, and possibly for backup in the tank." He doodled an abstract design only he could interpret. "Mikel, you realize this is not showgirl stuff we are doing." He turned the page on his tablet and looked me in the eyes. "We broke out of that Las Vegas pattern, girls made up like bejeweled-and-feathered mannequins descending staircases to pair-up with tuxedoed guys flaunting their homosexuality."

I bristled, but needed the job. I felt better when he described the concept of his *revolutionary* show.

Eyes lowered to his pencil, he continued, "Our performers create their own personal style, like you see on the streets of New York and other major cities. They become competitive, much like the Olympic athletes you've observed first hand in Los Angeles in '84 and again in Korea last year."

Jeff had done his homework since I called for an appointment. I remembered a young Cuba Gooding break dancing in the '84

Olympic closing ceremonies. I refused to be flattered. If anything, his shifty eye contact reminded me of Jaime Rogers, and I felt uncomfortable alone with him in the room with the door closed.

"Are you up for the challenge?"

"Yes." If I couldn't have *Jubilee*, I may as well try hip-hop and hard-core street dancing. Back at Debbie Reynolds Studio, Jaime pushed modern jazz and I could make the transition.

I would miss promenading across the stage in glamorous costumes, and I will always defend showgirl performance as an art form. However, in the future, my son would be spared any teasing about his mother going topless in public.

Outfitted in aquatic animal costumes like an octopus challenged my dignity, but I put on a good show. On a couple of occasions, I replaced the mermaid in the tank. I danced in a latticed metal globe, my routine followed by three motorcycles chasing each other around the circular floor and up the curved walls. Their precision was so exact, I could have kept dancing as they encircled me, but their roaring would have been intolerable. With a child in my life, I no longer courted dangerous situations.

What I didn't appreciate was Jeff Kutash's impertinence, calling at three in the morning wanting phone sex. Vince accused me of leading him on by flirting. I denied it but reconsidered. Comfortable with my red line, I knew my limits but my male associates might think otherwise. Where should I set my gray line between flirting and misleading? I doubt I will ever be able to lock it in place.

On a more positive note, I met Buddy Ebsen while at the Rivera, Nancy replaced by Dorothy Knott, young enough to be his daughter, clinging to his arm. I had done some research on early Buddy Ebsen movies as well as Gene Nelson's.

I reminded him, "You might not remember, but you were one of my first customers at Love's Barbeque in 1982. Since then, I watched you dance in *Broadway Melody of 1938* with Judy Garland and *Captain January* with Shirley Temple."

He blushed and said, "Even your mother would have been too young to have seen those movies."

CHAPTER 22

Nicholas, Vince, and I drove to Albuquerque for Christmas with my extended family, some members having yet to meet my son. Mom and Caroline flew to California the previous Yule season; *The Three Musketeers* never missed being together over the holidays.

Mother Nature blessed us with a flurry of snowflakes as we arrived. Bundled in his spaceman snowsuit, Nicholas nearly broke free from Vince's arms jerking this way and that to catch the flakes on his tongue.

I sprawled out on the inch of fresh snow in Mom's front yard. "Let's make angels." I fanned my arms and legs.

Nicholas squirmed loose from Vince and plopped on my stomach. "'gain, Mom." With each plop, I'd swing my arms and legs as if he had hit the switch. I laid him on his back and pressed his belly. After three or four attempts, he learned the angel-making procedure, waddling to fresh snow, plopping down, and yelling for me to press his belly. His angels and giggles caught attention from the house, Mom and Caroline rushing out to greet us.

My son claimed all the presents under the tree as his, more interested in their colorful wrapping then the contents when the bulk of them had been dished out to him. He quickly sorted the toys from clothing and other items, and soon fell sound asleep clutching his Teddy Bear with the blue and white striped baseball cap from Grandma.

By the end of our stay, tension developed between Mom and Vince over child-rearing techniques. An adherent of Dr. Spock, she preferred parents' coddling to strict discipline. When raising Caroline and me, she relegated discipline to Church-of-Christ doctrine, hour-long doses twice a week.

Vince had bonded with our son. He made stern but loving eye contact whenever Nicholas acted up, as much as a one-year-old could misbehave.

Mom would pull Nicholas into her arms and say things like, "Did Daddy scold? Is Daddy mean?" I knew it burned Vince, and I told Mom to stop. I approved the way Vince handled Nicholas. It set him on the right foot in life. Later, Mom would spoil both her grandsons, but Vince had already established Nicholas' personality.

Settling into a routine of doing *Splash* at the Riviera and Business Theater with Joe Morris, the gap in Vince and my relationship widened. He became secretive about his daily routine, his response to my questioning him, "Just trying to make a living." Any comment about his flirting with clients would earn the slam-dunk retort, "You should talk."

Both our careers involved mingling with the opposite sex, so I consciously shared all my social encounters, while he became more and more closed-mouth about his.

I always considered private investigation as a back-up career, so I purchased a recorder that could tap into our phone line. In a conversation with an old friend back East planning a vacation in Myrtle Beach, I heard, "Remember to bring lots of condoms." It might have been a joke, but I had suspected he was cheating on me, or at least wanting to go elsewhere for sex.

I overlooked the possibility of a separation, because our son would be entering the *terrible two's* stage in his development.

Nicholas needed a male influence, and my career took much of my time. Vince and I shared supervision, so Nicholas was never out of parental care.

I came home after *Splash* one night and found both the men in my life asleep, the small one on the lap of the full-grown one, and my heart softened. I laid Nicholas in his crib and let Vince sleep on his chair. A fun-loving kid, Nicholas would hide all scrunched in the bottom dresser drawer covered with Vince's clothes. He was and still is a charmer.

When driving into the parking lot at our apartment one night, through the rear view mirror, I spotted a creepy-looking guy running toward me. Our community wasn't gated, but we lived in a rather nice neighborhood west of the Strip. He had no business there. I paused to consider driving off, but caught sight of Vince's parked car. I felt safe enough to jump out and run up to our apartment.

Opening the door, I yelled, "There's a man following me. He's still outside staring."

"Are you sure?" Vince sounded annoyed by my interrupting him and his brother from back East.

"Of course I'm sure."

He got up from the couch, came to the door, and repeated, "Are you sure?"

That pissed me off, as if I merely wanted attention away from his brother. "Go out and let him know I don't live here alone."

I watched them approach the guy—thankfully they didn't shake hands—but they carried on a conversation like they were old buddies.

They returned, Vince with his *problem solved* expression. "He wasn't following you. Seemed like a nice fellow. Just lost. He got into his van and drove off."

"You let him get away?" *Strike three*, my caution-umpire sounded in my head. "He will be back. I know a stalker when I see one."

"Hold your temper, we got his license number."

We gave the number to my friend, Anthony, an officer in the Las Vegas Metropolitan Police Department. He said, "We'll check it out." He leaned closer. "In the meantime, Mikel, I advise you to purchase a gun. Las Vegas is not a very safe city."

The idea shocked me, never being around firearms. "Like what kind?"

He pondered the question and then tapped his holster. "I think you could handle a .38 caliber. Vince can help you pick one out."

My instinct proved to be correct. The guy was later charged peeping into bedroom windows.

I had enough bad things happen to me going back as far as high school. I began looking for a safer community to raise my son. Between a regular salary from *Splash* and various contracts with Business Theater, I could make the payments, even if Vince decided to return to California. I conferred with Ramona, my line captain from *Jubilee* who also did real estate, and signed the purchase agreement on a condominium.

"You made a decision just like that without even discussing it with me?" Vince's anger was worse than I expected. Like I needed his permission when spending my money.

"I have to get out of this neighborhood." I held eye contact. "Nicholas and I are moving to my new condo next month. For my son's sake, you can join us."

"What do you mean, no longer as a couple?"

"That shouldn't be news to you. We haven't communicated honestly with each other for a long time." My voice quivered. "Even if you don't join us, you can spend as much time with Nicholas as you want."

"I'm to be your male nanny? No way." His feelings had been hurt.

"Nicholas loves you and I probably do, too." I kept eye contact. "We can't continue our relationship with this wedge between us."

He didn't ask, and I didn't explain our elephant-in-the-room. He moved with us, but our relationship deteriorated further. Within a few months, he returned to California and then resettled back East. We still communicate and I consider him a friend. Although Nicholas can barely remember back that far, I made sure he understood the positive effect Vince had on his development.

Except for auditions and other job searches, my work hours took place at night, freeing me to spend most of the day with Nicholas. Helena, my neighbor from England, watched him when I was away. I only missed about three hours of my son's waking time, but I regretted not being there to bathe and tuck him in at bedtime.

I usually came home right after each performance, but Helena would stay late whenever I went clubbing with friends or cast members. I remained receptive but never desperate to meet the right man to share my life. Like my father, I felt most comfortable when in an committed relationship.

CHAPTER 23

Shortly before Vince moved away, I decided to audition for *Siegfried and Roy.* The pair of magicians had been performing in Las Vegas since 1967, starting at the Tropicana and moving to the old MGM Grand (years before I danced in *Jubilee*), to the Stardust, to the Frontier, and scheduled to open February 1990, on a twenty-five-million-dollar stage in their own showroom at the Mirage Hotel and Casino. I eagerly accepted the job, but how should I break the news to Jeff Kutash that I would be quitting *Splash*?

With Nicholas in my arms, I approached Jeff in his office mid-morning. He would be up and probably not yet on a rampage with dancers and technicians. He greeted me with a smile and gave my son a *coo-chi-coo* cheek-pinch. Nicholas eyed him suspiciously.

"I'm here to give my two-week notice that I am resigning. I've enjoyed—"

"You can't do that, Mikel. We have a contract."

"The six months will be up in two weeks."

"It has an extension at both of our discretions."

"Yes, and I am choosing to terminate the contract."

"*Siegfried and Roy*. I'm aware of what you've been doing." He tried another approach. "I could sue them for luring you away from the Riviera. There are ethics in show business."

I stood my ground without giving up my trump card. "Lynette Chappell, their business manager, informed me of my rights." I trusted the former Bluebell dancer, now Siegfried and Roy's *levitated* assistant, her body cut in half nightly on stage.

"We'll see." He turned as if to walk away.

I upped the ante. "I'll bet there are people who would like to know who you call at three in the morning demanding phone sex."

"I don't know what you are talking about." Jeff swung around, his body making contact with my son's clinched fist. Not yet two years old, Nicholas defended Mom.

Jeff dramatically ripped up my contract, and I couldn't wait to begin *Siegfried and Roy* rehearsals in a warehouse that replicated the Mirage stage still under construction.

***

Lynette Chappell's eyes roved between the group of sixty eager faces. "And Mikel."

My name, the last of eight called out. My heart pounded. Whatever the project, we would form the core. I loved the companionship that developed within small groups.

"You gals look like you're capable of routines requiring physical strength."

My initial reaction, I hope not more fifty-pound headgear or eight octopus legs sprouting from my body suit.

"Each of you will lead a group of eight soldier-dancers."

The image triggered a drum major leading a marching band. But why the extra strength requirement?

"You will control the movements of seven life-sized soldier puppets." She introduced us to our squads setting off stage. Four mechanical soldiers were loosely attached to a portable rack, two on either side of a slot for the control dancer. Above, three more puppets dangled from poles attached to the same contraption, all fixed to a skid.

"Take your positions and see if you can drag your units toward the stage."

The eight of us cautiously stepped into each *command center*, checked out the mechanism, and gave a shove.

"Why not put this on wheels?" Had the girl thought ahead, she could have realized wheels would make the unit unstable and her even asking suggested her hesitation.

"Can you do it?" The girl's comment nearly got her dropped from the routine.

The eight of us lugged our *Puppet Army* onto the stage, and we formed two lines spreading from the *Dragon's Mouth*, a fiery furnace where Siegfried did his disappearing act.

The soldiers' bodies were skeletal with hinged arms and legs, their gyrations coordinated by parallel bars strung between them. Handgrips gave me control of their movements; up and down, back and forward, left and right. I worked the bars to make my tin soldiers follow my dance step, their arms and legs dangling. Eight dancers and fifty-six soldiers performed *The Dance of the Puppet Army.*

The incident with the tiger breaking loose occurred during a rehearsal. Alone on stage, I stared straight ahead, as the tiger paused a few feet in front of me. I didn't need that last bit of advice to stand perfectly still. I was petrified. A whispered roar, or a rumbling purr, or a snort and a shrug, and the cat brushed past me. The heat radiating off his fur and his musty odor lingered, but I refused Siegfried's offer to take a break. The show must go on. The memory that stuck with me probably forever was the immense size of the animal, as big as *Barysh* before being pressed to pancake-size by a junkyard car crusher.

Tigers ate steak, dancers just hamburgers from the caterer. Both Siegfried and Roy treated their tigers well, often playing with them between acts. Roy let me hold a pair of cubs shortly after they were born, smaller than my poodle and just as playful. Every time I visited Venita and Chava, I was tempted to take *Nikov* back with me, but he had a good home.

Kenneth Feld, producer of *Disney on Ice* and *Ringling Brothers and Barnum and Bailey Circus*, turned the Mirage backstage into a mini Roman Coliseum. The facility accommodated lions, leopards, panthers, cheetahs, and their famous white tigers. And, an elephant. According to Siegfried, never a rabbit. Rather than pull a bunny from a hat, he made a much larger animal disappear in front of the audience. The elephant and its keeper lived in special accommodations on site, while the other animals resided at Siegfried and Roy's one hundred-acre *Little Bavaria*.

Kenny Rogers came to Vegas to introduce *Kenny Rogers Roasted Chicken* at the MGM Amusement Park, and he appeared as the first featured guest of *Siegfried and Roy*. While Kenny was in town, Vince and I took Nicholas to the amusement park, and we tried out Kenny Rogers Chicken. I told Kenny that we liked it better than Kentucky Fried. He chuckled and posed for a picture.

Stars from all over came to see the show and to be a part of it. Michael Jackson was a best friend to Siegfried and Roy, and he usually arrived for Roy's birthday celebration. Siegfried enjoyed showering Roy with little gifts and big surprises.

Roy celebrated his forty-fourth birthday October 3, 1990, the official date of Germany's reunification. He claimed it as, "A birthday present to me from the German people." Neither of them ever forgot their German heritage, as reflected in their accents.

Siegfried invited a surprise guest to Roy's forty-fifth birthday party. He let the cast in on the secret and allowed each of us to invite one person. I sent my mother a plane ticket to come for the show and to meet Siegfried and Roy, not mentioning the surprise celebrity.

I had told Siegfried about my mother's fascination with his guest, and he arranged for us to have a choice seat at the party. When Mom and I arrived, he came over to meet her. She maintained her composure and said, "Thank you, Siegfried. It's been a pleasure meeting you," her composure reminding me that she had mingled with celebrities in the past.

A different story when I said, "Mom, you better turn around. Someone else wants to meet you."

Elizabeth Taylor had entered the room from behind. Mom's face dropped and her body turned limp. Betty Jeanne maintained composure through my introduction, but with her idol gently touching her arm, she lost her voice. I wondered if Miss Taylor recognized her *White Diamonds* scent that Mom always wore.

Siegfried and Roy loved their moms and often showered them with gifts. I felt proud to give my mom the experience of meeting her idol, and I enjoyed buying her beautiful things. She had a taste for diamond jewelry, and she loved to shop at Neiman Marcus. She sacrificed a lot raising my sister and me, and I wanted to make her feel beautiful. She had been the best-dressed woman of Albuquerque, and I wouldn't let her forget it.

Siegfried and I shared a birthday, June 13, but his parties were never as elaborate as Roy's were. Liza Minnelli and Dolly Parton showed up on two separate occasions to join in the celebration. One other dancer from the show had that lucky birthday, and she, too, was invited. I danced with Siegfried, and he selected me for his disappearing act on stage. I think Lady Lynette resented all the attention he lavished on me.

Computers controlled Lights, the lifts, and anything mechanical, except my dragging the tin soldiers onto the stage and controlling their movements. It was cool. We performed under a huge dome, all electronics and mechanicals controlled by a computer. One time it shut down during a show, and all the dancers were stuck on stage, dome closed and music off. A dancer yelled, "Five-six-seven-eight…" We picked up the beat and kept dancing without music to the end of that number. They put a hold on the show to fix the problem. What a great experience that was.

One night after the late performance, Maureen, our dance captain, called the *Puppet Army* dancers aside and handed us each an envelope. She said, "I'm sorry."

Her sadness could only mean that she knew its contents and the information was bad. After a quick change into street clothes, I escaped to my car, a place of safety and solitude. Under the dome-light, I tore open the sealed document, and a single half-sheet of paper slid out and onto my lap. I stared into the windshield-turned mirror and immediately clicked off the dome light. I anticipated being fired and didn't want to watch my reaction. I balled the sheet of paper into my fist and drove to my condo.

Helena, my neighbor and nanny, flinched when I walked through the door with my face scowling and my hand in a fist. "How was Nicholas tonight? Did he go to bed okay?" My spirit brightened, and I tossed the wadded paper into the wastebasket as if it was some unwanted solicitation left outside my door.

"He fussed about an hour ago, so I warmed him some milk. He went right back to sleep."

I glanced at my watch and calculated back an hour. My son had sensed something bad happened at that exact time. I immediately perked up. He will not wake up in the morning to find his mother stressed.

I said, "Soon my schedule will change from nighttime to regular day hours, at least for a little while. Will you be available?"

"I'm busy during the day."

"That's okay. I can take Nicholas with me. But, nothing changes for the time being."

She left and I dug through the basket to see how much time I had to find a new job. Two weeks. I slept sound.

***

After two years of my never missing a performance, an executive (*Evil Queen*) decision replaced all twelve of us whose main job description was to perform the *Dance of the Puppet Army* without explanation. Dancers had little job protection. Rumor had it that some of the girls complained about being used as stagehands. Another speculation that we were paid more than the other dancers but less than the stage crew, and both groups used us to their benefit in contract negotiations. One glaring fact stood above all others, Vegas had a ready supply of especially female talent, and dancers can be replaced on a whim. I believe that was the case at *Siegfried and Roy.*

I never blamed Siegfried or Roy for the decision. I can envision Siegfried asking, "What happened to my Mikel. I need her for my disappearing act."

Lady Lynette responding, "You have plenty of others to choose from."

I won't say Lynette made the decision, but I am sure she approved and maybe even felt good about it.

During my tenure with the show, there were not any serious accidents or mishandling of the animals. I read somewhere that Siegfried suffered injuries requiring eighty-two stitches during his thirteen years at the Mirage. He supposedly said, "When I am standing there covered with blood, I know that I am going to get a standing ovation." I never witnessed any blood, his or others, on the stage.

Montecore, the tiger who attacked Roy, was not yet born when I danced in the show. On social media, Roy Horn recently posted the following message: *It is with great sorrow that I am writing you this note today that on March 19, 2014, in the early afternoon our beloved 17-year-old white tiger friend and brother, Montecore, left us and is now with his siblings in white tiger heaven.*

Montecore died a month after Mom attended her daughter's last showgirl performance in "Sassy" at age fifty. Tigers in captivity can live from fifteen to twenty-five years, about the performing range for a Vegas showgirl. Retired tigers perform for the public at Siegfried & Roy's Secret Garden habitat at the Mirage. Retired showgirls resort to second careers spread throughout the community.

CHAPTER 24

After leaving *Siegfried and Roy*, I accepted a dancing job in Jose Nurbair's *Cabaret Circus* at the Lady Luck Hotel and Casino. Our outfits ranged from colorful Mardi Gras celebration to cowgirl, leather chaps replaced by fluffy white and black pantaloons with sleeves to match. We had an oriental costume and, over-the-top to my notion, we dressed as clowns and even as pairs of dice running and tumbling across the stage. Not my favorite show, but I reunited with some of my old *Jubilee* friends like Jackie and Marla and Svetlana, a gal from Russia. Marla took a break from her career after giving birth to triplets, and I thought one child was a handful. Male dancers made up about a third of the cast of a couple dozen. A small show, we dressed in back lot trailers and performed in an air-conditioned tent.

Dad and Judy came to celebrate Nicholas's fourth birthday. Their grandson performed for them all afternoon, and I did the same that evening at Lady Luck. My girlfriends swarmed around Dad like he was Xavier Cugat, the Cuban-American bandleader whom he did resemble.

The show lasted until tickets stopped selling. Three years before the city constructed a lighted canopy over five blocks of Freemont Street, all the downtown casinos had been struggling. Lady Luck was located on a side street away from most foot traffic.

Despite my setback with *Siegfried and Roy*, the four years between my return to Vegas from California and the implosion of the Dune's Hotel in 1993 continued to be a productive and happy period of my life. Mom remained in good health and spent part of each year in Vegas with her grandson and part back home with Jim and Church-of-Christ friends. Caroline's clinic was prospering and she had settled into a solid domestic relationship with Cindy, and my older brothers and sisters were comfortable in their careers. Dad and Judy, who married when they came to watch me perform in *Jubilee*, enjoyed an active life on a Texas ranch.

Most important, I had Nicholas to nurture and watch grow in a safe and healthy environment at my condominium. I was able to pay down my mortgage while working *Siegfried and Roy* and doing six to eight Business Theater productions each year.

I missed Vince but kept too busy to dwell on our separation. Although he and Mom never saw things eye-to-eye, her increased visits did not drive him away. We had our issues. Nicholas loved sharing his bedroom with Grandma. He would sleep in an upper bunk with my mother below him. She made up for the loss of his pal he called *Daddy*.

I enrolled Nicholas in karate and soccer as early as possible, thinking sports would develop agility and stamina and coaches would provide a male influence. For his artistic development, he participated in dancing, acting, and modeling classes.

Those of us who went through the pregnancy boom put our babies and toddlers in a commercial for Kids' Camp at Maryland Square Shopping Center. A former dancer owned the children's clothing and furniture store, and we both participated with our children in the advertising. We gathered in back yards and parks for picnics and birthday parties and hired or created entertainment for the kids. A stagehand from *Jubilee* dressed up like a dinosaur from *Jurassic Park* as a surprise guest. We would tie in current children's themes seen on television and take advantage of holiday hoopla. I printed Christmas cards with pictures of Nicholas in his Sunday best hand-in-hand with his mom in showgirl headdress.

After eight years, Business Theater began to slow down, and when it ended, I had been prepared. The day I received my pink slip from *Siegfried and Roy*, I felt the world had caved in, but I picked myself up, brushed myself off, and began to audition the next day.

Traditional Vegas began to crumble; hotels along the strip imploded to reopen bigger and better, as dictated by financial statements. Profit-conscious corporations replaced the face of the mob; no more casually bumping shoulders with the Spilotro brothers and other mobsters at the Botany Club.

When I performed at *Jubilee*, a similar focus on costs ended the live music. The orchestra pit converted to a table seating area created revenue. With the orchestra back stage and out of view, its artistic effect had been lost. No one but the musicians would feel the negative impact from switching to recorded music, positive effects on the corporation's bottom line.

Thanks to Michael Pratt and Fluff LeCoque and Diane Palm for preserving *Jubilee*, but how much longer can Bally's hold out? Everyone should see the show while it's still here. I am so happy I came to Vegas at the right time to be a part of the most wonderful and beautiful shows in the world. It opened the door to my wide and varied career as an entertainer in Las Vegas.

People loved the old Vegas, especially locals, but our numbers could not keep up with the influx of tourists. Russian gymnasts like my neighbor, Tatiana, set a new style of performance in *Cirque du Soleil* set to open at the Riviera by the end of 1993. The production had an existing cast with no options for traditional showgirl dancers to audition.

When Jeff Kutash asked me to rejoin the *Splash Company* on tour in Japan, I broke the bad-things-always-happen-in-threes syndrome. He booked Nicholas as part of David Copperfield's illusion act. A few years earlier in China, Copperfield made their Great Wall disappear, so I assumed he could make my preschool kid disappear in Japan, and he had better make him reappear. I saw an opportunity to give Nicholas some serious karate training in the art of defense as the Japanese intended.

We had all necessary travel documents and our bags packed, when Jeff cancelled our part of the act. Kutash, a former Golden Glove champion, probably remembered being sucker-punched by a toddler and worried what Nicholas with karate training could do to him. I allowed Jeff the benefit of the doubt. When David Copperfield's act fell through—assuming it ever had been negotiated—he no longer had a role for my son, and Jeff knew I would not go without him. However, he should have given us more than a day's warning.

Everything worked out for the best, because the tour was cut short due to Jeff's personal and financial problems. Nicholas and I might have been stranded with our bags packed at Narita International Airport in Tokyo forced to find our own way back home.

With the inevitable third bad thing behind us, I picked up the pieces from the loss of three shows and Jeff Kutash throwing us to the curb. No problem; if a dance position opened up, I would seize it. Already back in grade school, I went for the Thanksgiving turkey, and since then, I hadn't missed any goal I set for myself.

A touch of traditional Vegas survived in showrooms at Stardust, Bally's, Tropicana, and The Dunes not yet knocked down to emerge with a different species of entertainment inside mega hotels.

My next conquest, *Wild Things*.

CHAPTER 25

Caroline raised her glass and scanned the faces around my small condo kitchen—Mom, Suzanne and her daughter, Candice, Nicholas, and me. She announced, "Here's to *Wild Things*, an appropriate show for my wild sister."

We cheered and Nicholas banged his spoon on his plate. I needed to dignify the show at the Dunes Hotel and Casino with some name-dropping. Choreographed by Michael Darrin brought nods and smiles. Breck Wall and Patrick Maes, two famous movie directors, received nods of possible recognition from Suzanne and Candice, probably reacting to their experience with directors on the movie set for *Honeymoon in Vegas* where I got them walk-on parts.

Mentioning Kirby Van Burch and Bobby Berosini, a glimmer of interest spread across my mother's face. I explained, "Clyde, Berosini's orangutan, appeared with Clint Eastwood in *Every Which Way but Loose*."

Mom made a connection. "Isn't that the orangutan that his trainer beat to death because Clint Eastwood didn't like him?"

Clint Eastwood was one of the leading men in her repertoire of male movie stars. "It wasn't true, Mom. Clyde died shortly after the filming in1978, and that horrible rumor took off. Bobby told me about it."

Berosini had a reputation as a stern animal trainer, and I didn't tell her that a couple of my dancer friends from *Enter The Night* at the Stardust filed a complaint with *People for the Ethical Treatment of Animals*, one of the reasons Bobby moved his act to the Dunes. I had to change my attitude toward showgirls performing in the same venue as animals, especially orangutans. Primates have as much dignity as white tigers, as I discovered working with Berosini. I enjoyed sharing the stage with him, and Nicholas loved to play with a young orangutan.

Mom changed the subject. "Apes on the job and a monkey at home." She tickled Nicholas and he giggled.

"Your grandson-monkey doesn't stay home, Mom. At least not all the time." An opportunity to bring out the photo album. "I just happen to have a picture of him with his little orangutan friend."

I passed around the snapshot of Nicholas side-by-side with an adolescent orangutan, both the same size, Nicholas in jeans and country shirt and the orangutan wearing a white robe.

Candace said, "Aunt Mikel, I can hardly wait to see your show tomorrow."

Suzanne said, "Yes, and we thank you for the complimentary passes to *Wild Things*, my wild sister."

We glanced at my smirking sister, Caroline, and chuckled. They didn't need to know that I paid for their tickets.

***

I experienced the opening of three new shows, *Cabaret Circus*, *Siegfried and Roy*, and *Wild Things*; *Jubilee* and *Splash* had been ongoing when I joined the casts, different advantages to either situation. Shows in progress demanded my attention to details and fitting in, while new shows required patience as the directors and set designers paid attention to the details. With the four costume changes in *Wild Things*, I spent hours under the hot lights working on the dance sequences, often just listening to choreographers and musical directors assert themselves. As a lowly cast member, I could only hope their decisions would enhance rather than overtax my talent.

If this were to be my last hurrah as a dancer/showgirl, I could claim it as a peak experience, second only to *Jubilee*. No clowns or human dice rolling across the stage and no operating mechanical soldiers, just live performers, most of them human beings. The less-than-human, one snake, a few orangutans, and sometimes choreographer Michael Darrin who demanded the nearly impossible from us. For instance: on a count of four, jumping onto a stack of three-foot cubes and striking a pose at the top. It was do or die, as the first girl who attempted and failed discovered.

"Next!" No doubt, her audition came to an abrupt end.

Red faced, Michael glanced my way. "Mikel, can you do it?"

"I can do it." Challenges surfaced from the depth of my past, the turkey trot, cheerleading tryouts, and ice-skating on demand. I walked around the stack reviewing every angle.

Under his breath, Michael muttered, "You don't get to pick which side to start."

By then I had attempted the jump at least three times in my mind, quite sure the last one completed the sequence. I needed the rhythm to set the pattern of which beat to be at what level, and how much spring action to add at each pivot point. Most critical would be striking a pose on the fourth count, not struggling for balance or falling off the backside.

"Are you going to do it or not, Mikel?" Darrin scowled

Fired up by his challenge, I said, "Give me the count."

Michael's grin broke free, and he snapped his fingers.

I lodged about a dozen beats in my head and charged up the pyramid of boxes, perfect pivot on each with only a slight teeter at the top. I struck my pose and mouthed a quiet *thank you* to Jaime Rogers for hard training.

"That's your new spot. You got the *Zebra on the Box*."

We did a jazzy number, *Cold Hearted Snake*, from Paula Abdul's album *Forever Your Girl*, her video inspired by Bob Fosse's *All That Jazz*. Such a notorious musical history challenged Michael Darrin's creativity and our dance talent to do it justice. We did and it felt wonderful.

In my provocative *Scaffold* routine, a combination of bur-lesque poles and monkey bars, my body slithered, played peek-a-boo—heavy on the peek—and shimmied up and down; did chin-ups, push-ups, and squats in equal measure. I played ring-around-the-pole, my body an arrow or a ray gun scanning the showroom.

In *Bolero*, graceful orchestra music introduced female dancers in pairs, and we did our showgirl walk across the stage, white knee-high boots with heels and a black and gold ruffled train over our shoulders. As a prop, an unlit cigarette in a long slender holder tucked between finger and thumb like sophisticated ladies from a 1920's speakeasy.

After my family's gushing oohs and aahs over my performance, Mom said, "Mikel, you shouldn't smoke."

Topless okay, smoking not okay. Mom had her priorities.

CHAPTER 26

Happy fifth birthday, Nicholas Bryce Peterson.

Four days later, at two AM on October 27, 1993, I stood on Las Vegas Boulevard and witnessed what a ton of explosives and four thousand gallons of aviation fuel could do to the Dunes Hotel.

"Captain of the Britannia, are you ready, sir?"

"Aye, aye, Captain."

"Prepare broadside. Ready! Aim! Fire!" The British ship commissioned for entertainment at the adjacent Treasure Island Hotel added a bit of theater. Thank you Steve Wynn for giving me *Siegfried and Roy* at the Mirage but not for taking away *Wild Things*, the show that died with the Dunes to a cheering crowd of two-hundred-thousand on-lookers. In its place, came the Bellagio where dancing fountains replaced dancing showgirls.

The Dune's demise was spectacular, my career more personal, probably my last opportunity to perform in a major Las Vegas showroom. Oddly, the smoldering ashes revived my optimism. Nothing can stop Mikel!

I rushed back to my condo to relieve Helena, whom I might not be able to afford much longer. Forgoing my ritual of winding down with a glass of wine and a hot bubble bath, I kissed my sleeping son, tucked his Teddy bear with the blue and white striped baseball cap under his arm, and went to bed. Alone.

The morning following the Dunes destruction, I awoke sharing my pillow with a Teddy bear that had not been there when I went to bed only a couple of hours earlier. It didn't arrive on its own, but tossing back the sheets produced no five-year-old.

"Nicholas?" I grabbed my robe and headed toward the kitchen. "Nicholas, Honey."

"I'm out here, Mom."

Kneeling on a chair with bowl, cereal box, and carton of milk on the table in front of him, my son waved me a *good morning* with a dripping spoon. "Hi. I made my own breakfast."

I grabbed a paper towel and dabbed at a few wet spots on table, chair, and boy. "Good morning, Sweetie." I brushed his cowlick down.

"I kissed your forehead. Told you I could get my own breakfast. Teddy stayed to watch you sleep."

I sat alongside him, poured cereal into the bowl he had set for me, and added milk. I picked the bowl up with both hands and pretended to drink from it.

"That's not the right way to eat cereal, Mom."

"Well, you didn't supply me with a spoon."

"You can have mine when I'm done."

"You just finish eating." I rose but settled back down and marveled at my competent young man. By the time he finished and handed me his spoon, I knew what my next project would be.

My sister's response when I called later that morning, "Have you discussed your idea with Mom and Jim?" In other words, will they back me financially? Caroline had recently opened her own clinic in Dayton, Ohio, and she had shared step-by-step the complex and costly process.

"It's only a dance studio for children, not the opening of a hospital."

"It's just a clinic, not a hospital, but a big enough step." She paused, and I resisted overselling my idea too quickly. "Sorry, Mikel, but I have to run. Check with dance studios in your area and gather as much information as possible. When we get together at Christmas, we can discuss a number of issues."

"Yeah, thanks. Love you."

"Love you, too."

Two months until the holidays. I needed to act.

With a list of studios from the Yellow Pages and newspaper ads, my son and I set out to investigate each pretending an interest in his enrolling. Unaware of my actual intention, Nicholas objected to dance classes until an instructor asked what kind of sports he liked.

He shouted, "Karate," and did his Ninja Turtle pose.

She responded, "Dance lessons develop universal skills including karate moves."

"I can break-dance, too, but I don't need lessons."

"That's interesting. I have a few students who do that sort of street stuff while waiting for class to begin."

That sort of street stuff? Waiting for class to begin? I recalled Cuba Gooding's break-dance routine already back during the closing ceremony at the '84 Olympics. Has this woman been living under a rock?

"My cousins and me take turns showing Grandpa Lesmen and Grandma Judy what we can do. Sometimes they tell me I did the best." He glanced at me as if expecting to be corrected for boasting.

I let him know I approved. "Tell her about the older kids you had to show how to do it." He blushed. Had I embarrassed him? Not Nicholas.

"'Member, Mom, when that big kid tried to copy me, and he fell on his butt?" He giggled, and I shushed him. Pride is one thing, but gloating is something else.

I decided on the spot that break dancing would be a part of my program. I interrupted their conversation before Nicholas accidentally exposed our intentions. I learned a lot from listening to studio personnel pitch a five-year-old on the idea of dance class. After the fourth or fifth interview, Nicholas softened his resistance to taking dance classes, so I cut the interviews short or face his disappointment for not signing up.

If I were to rate the dance studios we visited, most would earn a c-minus based on the externals. I hadn't observed Nicholas involved in an actual dance lesson, but the environment of each studio did little to support a creative atmosphere. In one case, parents sat behind a curtain unable to watch their children perform. Some hadn't a wooden floor, so important to absorb and dissipate or return body movement. A floor without some give and spring would be hard on the knees and ankles.

On our way back home, we stopped across from the rubble that had been the Dunes.

Nicholas asked, "What happened, Mommy?"

"Just like in the Bible story, the walls came tumbling down." His expression remained inquisitive, but I allowed him to work it through. He either resolved the issue or passed it off as another adult-type confusion.

My walls continued to stand, but a wave of sadness washed over me. Where will Bobby Berosini take his orangutans? Like me, he must be feeling the pangs of a lost opportunity. He eventually moved his act to Branson, Missouri, and I stayed in Vegas to establish *Mikel's Performing Arts Academy*.

By Christmas, I had a business plan that included my choice of location and costs to make it a first class studio; floating wood floor, mirrored walls, and dance Barres all around. I included an estimate of the minimum number of students to turn a profit.

Caroline asked, "What's your strategy to attract students?"

Me! I can do that. Why would my sister doubt my ability to sell myself? On reflection, I responded, "Yellow Pages and newspaper ads. The same way I located studios to do my research."

Before anyone had a chance to ask where the money would come from, I said, "I could use the equity in my condo."

Caroline said, "How can there be any? You've only owned it five years."

"I made extra principal payments, and property values have gone up since 1989."

Mom shook her finger, "You don't touch that mortgage. I taught you that the roof over your head is the most important asset."

My trained body is my best asset, but the job-market for my skill is limited. Teaching would best utilize my talent. I drew a breath unsure how to state my case.

Caroline held up her hand. "Cindy and I are prepared to invest in our sister's project."

A sigh of relief. "Thank you. I love you so much! I won't let you down."

I combined my talent and training with my past involvement in an array of artistic programs to create a studio and miniature theater for children. I drew on lessons learned at Jeytte Sparlin's modern dance classes back in Albuquerque, with Jaime Rogers' hard core at Debbie Reynolds Studio, and from my modeling and dance experiences. I have a natural ability to communicate with children, a talent for costume and set design to enhance chore-ography and presentation, and salesmanship skills to convince parents to enroll their children. My program's goals; self-esteem and self worth for students, parents, and instructor.

Creating my dance studio resembled my pregnancy, the conception happened quickly, assembling all the pieces took nearly a year, but joy and relief at the grand opening made the process worthwhile. Thus, began the nurturing process to attain the studio's capacity of eighty to ninety children and dealing with even more parents.

I love teaching and helping my students develop the strength of a track runner, agility to perform various dance steps, and poise of a ballerina. Most important, have fun, cooperate, challenge the body, and learn to feel good about one's self. Appropriate slogans might be *music and movement* or *creative expression* or *challenge your God given talents.*

I divided the lessons into four groups defined by students' ages, 3-4, 5-6, 7-8, and pre-teens, classes meeting an hour a week. I scheduled myself from 3-6 o'clock daily for instruction and follow up projects.

With a facility larger than needed, I sublet mornings to adult classes for jazzercise, and evenings for ballroom dancing. Incorporating an acting emphasis gave *Mikel's Dance Studio* an additional creative edge and a new sign above the door, *Mikel's Performing Arts Academy.*

I recruited my friend, Jackie, from *Wild Things* to teach ballet, my strength being modern dance, jazz and tap. Nicholas objected to any participation with me as his instructor.

CHAPTER 27

Every family experiences crisis moments, none more serious than the death of a family member. While in the process of setting up my dance studio, I received the dreaded 1:30 AM phone call.

Mom's shaking voice, "Your brother, Jeffrey, passed away in his sleep moments ago."

I sat up stunned. His teasing from back when I was a teen entered my head and stuck there like plainsong. "My little sister, Michelle, you smelled like a stinky diaper." He composed that little ditty when he supposedly changed my diaper, not too likely with two older sisters in the family. I laughed through my tears. I would give anything to hear his chanting that tune again.

Personal issues brought him back to his family in Albuquerque from Quanah, Texas, where he was a roofer. I almost had him convinced to move to Las Vegas, and I could find him less strenuous work. Having a male family member around always made me feel safe. He had been a kind and loving brother who would take the shirt off his back and give it to anyone in need. At that point in his life, his need was Mom.

No mother should have to experience the loss of a child. I jumped out of bed, ran into Nicholas' room, and watched him breathe. Retreating to the kitchen, I sat at the table staring into my coffee. The phone rang.

"Hello, Caroline." We both sobbed.

***

People say that when you return to your childhood home, it appears smaller than you remember. Perhaps as children, everything seemed big, but in our mother's case, usable space in her house shrunk. She'd always been a collector of nice things, but recently her gathering of stuff bordered on hoarding. Spring catalogues began her three-season ordering of Christmas gifts, stored and often forgotten. An avid reader, she ordered more magazines than she could possibly read, so she marked articles of interest and set them aside. Included were tablets and notebooks titled with only a few entries of whatever piqued her interest at the moment.

Caroline casually suggested, "Mom, why don't you pack up and move to Las Vegas with Mikel and Nicholas? You spend half your time there anyway. It is just too much for you to keep up a house this size."

"Mikel's condo is too small for all my things." Topic dropped, end of story. *Her things* had taken control of her life. Only after reflection did she mentioned Jim and church friends as a reasons for staying in Albuquerque.

A year and a couple extended visits later, I sensed she might be warming up to a possible move. With the real estate section of the *Review Journal* under my arm, I asked, "Mom, want to come with Nicholas and me to look at some new homes in El Capitan Ranch? It's a residential development not far from here."

She cautioned, "Your business is still growing. You better save your money," but she grabbed her hat and sweater. "I suppose it doesn't hurt to look."

After walking through the model home and listening to the agent's sales pitch, Mom said, "I can loan you the deposit." Our deal was cinched.

In 1996, I leased my condo, and moved into a new three-bedroom home at 8781 Autumn Valley with a mortgage, something I hoped would be in my past forever. Mom agreed to leave Albuquerque, if she could convince Jim to give up his house and take an apartment in Las Vegas.

His response, "I can't abandon my bridge group. Betty Jeanne can visit you as often as she wants, but her place is here with us. Her friends need her."

Later, Jim became ill requiring an assisted living arrangement. He and Mom both agreed to take up residence in Vegas, Mom in her own home in El Capitan Ranch close to mine and Jim at a private nursing home nearby on Craig Avenue. Caroline negotiated all the financial matters, selling and buying Betty Jeanne's properties, buying her a car, and helping Jim dispose of his stuff. When everything settled, all of us who helped him move needed to be vaccinated against hepatitis-B, a small price to pay for all he had done for us.

With Mom's new house at 8760 Country Pines Avenue just around the corner, Nicholas liked the having Grams with us all year, but missed her sleeping in the bunk below him.

I said, "You're nine years old. You can cut through the back yards all by yourself whenever you want to visit Grandma." His eyes lit up.

Mom refused to give up any of her furniture, her random collection of beautiful things, and even the stacks of papers and magazines from her living room that nearly reached the ceiling. They filled her new house and half of her double garage, but she was happy. Had I to do it over, she would have moved in with me, which did happen a few years later.

CHAPTER 28

My teaching philosophy, *everyone a star;* give each student an opportunity to develop a two minute performance. Preparing for Dance Awards, each individual picked a favorite song, video, movie, or even a childhood fairy tale. They could choose from American themes of time and place like the cowboy west, Hollywood, and Bourbon Street. I would help choreograph the dance steps and offer suggestions for costumes and props.

"You look just like Barbie." Kids say the darndest things, but this six-year-old's comment was a set-up. We were doing a Hawaiian show, and the girl's mother had dressed a Barbie doll in a grass skirt over a tropical flower-design swimsuit, a rather creative hula costume.

"My Mom said this is for you. You look just like Barbie."

Hard to argue with such a gift, even if it turned out to be a bribe.

"My mother said you should put me in the center."

Aha! A teachable moment. "You are already near the center, but some of the girls are taller, and that's how dancers need to be arranged."

She accepted my explanation, and I even complimented her for being open-minded. However, during the performance, she shoved her way to center stage. Her action called for corrective measures. I talked to her mother who agreed that her daughter was a problem child, but a small curl of the mouth expressed her true feelings. I talked to the *problem child* who had the *problem mother*, and explained the etiquette dancers observe.

"You look like Barbie." The kid had a memorized one-liner, and she, or her mother, had found my Achilles heel. I am a dancer on and off stage. I maintain a trim body, good posture, and cheerful attitude. Often, I find little girls staring up at me with admiration. My smile attracts their attention, and I turn it into a positive by explaining how everyone can develop his or her God-given assets.

We did group hugs when someone felt left out, teacher included. Having a bad day? It's time for a group hug. With each class—yes, even the pre-teens—I would take a picture of intertwined bodies, smiling faces visible, to take home to parents. Pre-teens might show their friends, but I doubt parents ever saw them.

Although purchasing costumes was the parents' responsibility, I explained how to enhance their child's individual physique. Dancers should be proud of how they look as well as their performance on stage.

One little girl blurted, "My mother said you look much older than on your picture in the window." Darndest and truth-fullest words from a child. Comments like that keep my inner-Barbie humble.

Locating a stage on which to perform took some fancy footwork on my part, cajoling, bribing, and trading favors. I choreographed the play *Annie* at Palo Verde High School in exchange for use of their stage for recitals. The theater at Summerlin Library granted free use to community groups not charging admission, wages for a technician our only expense.

Mary Poppins was our most elaborate production. Nicholas and his friend, Kelli Crossley, played Jane and Michael. Girls dressed in frilly pink frocks with white hats, and the boys wore colorful shirts, knickers with suspenders, and white sailor caps. I supplied special ribbons to decorate hats and caps, and I bought a harness and a parasol for my flying onto the scene.

The smaller girls pointed and yelled their line. "Look, it's Mary Poppins." My friend from *Jubilee* who looked like Dick Van Dyke played the chimney sweep. I charcoaled everyone's arms and faces for the song and dance routine, "Step in Time" with Dick Van Dyke look-alike.

Supercalifragilisticexpialidocious from mouths with permanent teeth in various stages of development produced a song through which no parent could keep a straight face.

Students gave recitals, performed in the Magical Forest at Christmas, did Dance Awards, and participated in parades and half time at sports events. Our annual performance took place at Knott's Berry Farm in California. I encouraged parents to build a family vacation around their trip west, a chance to see their child perform in front of an audience of strangers. *Mikel's Performing Arts Academy* had possession of the open stage on the grounds for one hour, and we filled all the seats and standing room. Kids performing in costumes had a natural draw for families passing by.

With free passes for the remainder of the day, kids ran from attraction to attraction until they wore their parents out, me included.

Too big, too fast, a common business phenomenon I was to discover the hard way. To cover expenses, I had to rely on my other sources of income. I was about to throw in the towel and tell parents that *Mikel's Performing Arts Academy* would be shutting down.

A three-year-old girl tugged on my ballet skirt. "I love you, Miss Mikel"

That's it. I could not quit. I redoubled my efforts to earn extra income. Calling agents and working my network, I found jobs teaching dance, doing commercials and impersonations, modeling, and taking bit parts in movies.

Jamie, a friend and Dolly Parton impersonator from *An Evening at LaCage* at the Riviera, showed me how to make up my face to resemble Liza Minnelli. He squared off my nose and drooped my bottom lip and eyes with cosmetics. Put on a wig and, presto, Liza Minnelli. I studied her moves to impersonate her style of performance. I auditioned made-up to look like Liza for Encore Productions doing a commercial as a vacation destination. They filmed from the top of the Tropicana Hotel with the New York, New York Hotel in the background, me dancing and lip-syncing one of her songs.

I had helped my sister and niece, Suzanne and Candace, get walk-on parts in the movie *Honeymoon in Vegas* starring Nicholas Cage and Jessica Parker, and helped Caroline sign on as an extra during the filming of *Over the Top* with Sylvester Stallone. I was busy and couldn't audition for movies at the time, but I came by to watch. Meeting Sylvester Stallone face-to-face in a hallway, he stopped his bodyguards and stared at me.

He said, "I'm sorry, but I thought you were Susan Anton." He added, "My ex girlfriend," as if everyone hadn't heard about their affair and breakup. I knew our faces had a natural resemblance and this encounter cinched it. Sylvester posed for a picture with me, and I pursued an opportunity.

Susan Anton lived in Vegas and hosted *Great Radio City Music Hall Spectacular* at the Flamingo Hotel. She and her husband, Jeff Lester, opened their production company, *Big Pictures*, in 1997, about the time I was heavy into impersonations. I had my photographer, Evon, do my body shot posed like Susan Anton from the cover of *Shape Magazine*.

I presented the photos side-by-side to Susan and Jeff with a proposal to act as her stunt double whenever she did a movie. They marveled how much we looked alike and agreed to explore the possibilities of working together. I had hoped for a relationship where we could perform like Carol Burnett and Vicki Lawrence, but nothing developed.

I included Susan Anton in my repertoire and gave Marilyn Monroe space in my closet. Back in my days at *Jubilee*, a wardrobe lady-friend made a replica white dress from Marilyn Monroe's movie *Seven Year Itch* and her hot pink dress with bow and jewels from *Diamonds are a girl's best friend*. Whenever opportunity occurred like posing at a wedding chapel with a make-believe Elvis in a pink Cadillac, I would dress up as Marilyn. I perfected her "Happy Birthday Mr. President" popping out of a gift box with a huge bow on the cover. These impersonations were popular party gigs.

I also did a commercial for R&R Productions as the mother in a nerd family who stayed home instead of vacationing in Las Vegas. I came to the audition already dressed for the part. I wore an outdated and modest Sunday church-dress. I never throw out old outfits, not knowing what look some director might want. And, they all still fit! With my hair done up in a beehive like Marge from *The Simpsons*, I wore a pair of pointy glasses taped in the middle. On the drive to the set, my character stopped traffic. By time I arrived, I had the giggles, and my laughter was contagious with the filming crew.

The director said, "If you can act like Lucille Ball or Carol Burnett, you have the role."

I could and did. I was hyped. In small town America, two children played in a plastic kiddie's pool, husband and wife on lounge chairs near the street in front of the house reading the paper. Along came a truck and splashed mud all over them. The camera flashed ahead to a collage of people enjoying Las Vegas.

A voice-over, "Why stay at home when you could have this?"

In the final scene, mom and dad with their knees tucked under their chins sat squeezed into the pool with their kids standing by wearing sad expressions. In the early nineties, some hotels promoted Vegas as a family destination. Back then, *What happens in Vegas stays in Vegas* could have meant a dirty diaper.

Overall, I did dozens of commercials advertising products from dance studios, to fragrance, to fashion. Most important, I sold Mikel as the product, *Post Card Girl of Las Vegas*. I offered my image to promote shows, gift items, but without any copyright protection.

During one of her visits, Caroline called from her car all excited. "Your showgirl image covers the entire front side of Harrah's Hotel."

"I don't know what you're talking about."

"We were driving down the Strip and Nicholas yelled, 'That's my mom.' Cindy and I did a u-turn to take a second look."

"And?"

We're sure it's you. Come down and see for yourself."

Even with my face fogged, I recognized the picture of me surrounded with fan dancers on a permanent banner. I had a good idea who might have passed it on to the advertising company.

Center Point Productions cast me in some television shows including *Dreams* and *You Ruined My Life*. I felt proud to be cast in a *CSI* production at the Golden Nugget, swimming in their shark tank alongside bikini-clad teens who could have been my daughters. One of the characters was bitten and the water turned red to simulate blood. My skin took on a hue reminiscent of my sunburn experience during *City Lites*.

Much of my career depended on keeping my body in shape, and purposely not dressing to fit my age. When middle-aged female roles become the fad, I will adjust.

In the movie, *Mars Attack*, starring Jack Nicholson and Glenn Close, I was selected from the group to do an opening scene in a casino with Jim Brown. As the Cleveland Browns fullback stood off to the side and watched, I pulled the slot handle—they still had mechanical machines back then—and sevens came up. Michael J. Fox did a cameo role, but I didn't ask him about the stuffed moose Douglas Nelson and I gave him during the filming of *Teen Wolf.* I doubt he wanted to be reminded of that dud movie.

Nicholas and I earned bit parts in *Fools Rush In*, with Mathew Perry and Selma Halyek and he did a walk-on in *Mars Attack.* His major movie debut occurred a year later in *Pay It Forward* with Helen Hunt and Kevin Spacey. He was the official stunt stand-in for a member of the teen gang that accosted the main character. I settled for a-woman-in-the-crowd walk-on role.

A group of female musicians called *Sister Band* hired me to do their choreography. They had a lot of talent, but one of the girl's husband/manager never brought the members to the same page, and they fell apart. Too bad because they cut a well-received album.

Starting a tradition of showmanship at family birthday parties, I presented Cindy with my Marilyn Monroe impersonation. I set a fan under her replicated white dress for the blast of air to expose my panties. Caroline's partner claimed me as her wife and we joked and laughed about it.

More difficult to impersonate was Barbara Streisand, Caroline's favorite singer. My sister always did nice things for everyone, so I wanted to do something special on her birthday. I had a long pearl beaded cream-colored dress with a train that draped down the back. I applied makeup so drastic that nobody wanted to even get close to me. With a wig drooping down the sides of my cheeks and my eyes crossed, I descended the stairs with great class and fanfare.

Surrounded by family, Caroline whooped and hollered, "My little sister just pulled one off on me. For a split second, I believed Barbara Streisand had come to my birthday party."

Mom said, "Why not? Mikel had Elizabeth Taylor come to my mine."

"Mom, it was Roy Horn's party, and I didn't do the inviting."

She chuckled. "That's not the way I remember it. Elizabeth came to see me."

"Yeah, Mom, like you played cards on the train with Marlene Dietrich." I teased her into retelling that story.

She drew a deep breath. "On the first class coach to Los Angeles, Dr. Peterson and I were seated across from Marlene and her …."

She paused and Caroline finished her sentence. "*Friend*, Mom. Last time you changed it from *lover* to *friend*. When we were kids you always said Marlene and her *agent*."

"No, the agent was the man who made the TWA pilot turn his plane around to come back for me."

Mom checked eye contact with everyone in the room. "I explained my situation to the ticket agent and went to the Fred Harvey Restaurant and Lounge to have a drink in the Ernest Blumenthal Terminal building. Dr. Peterson and Ernest were good friends back in '39 when he designed it. A few years later, my husband and I flew our Cesena from that terminal. The building's on the Historical Register now."

Another scan of family members. "There were two doors, north facing the parking lot and the exit to the taxiway to the south. Suddenly a huge silver nose with the red letters *TWA* in a red circle glided into view. Over the public address came, 'Mrs. Betty Jeanne Peterson, please report to the ticket gate.' Ground crew pushed the portable stairs to the rear door of the plane, and I strutted through the passenger area to the first class section. Of course, I was dressed to the nines, so I looked important enough to turn a plane around. By coincidence, my seat was next to Dr. Peterson's accountant, and we both had a good chuckle over it."

Leave it to my mother to upstage my Barbra Streisand birthday surprise.

CHAPTER 29

The mother of one of my students approached me with an unusual request. "I'm a pole dancer, and I need some advice." Pole, vertical, not horizontal like the Barres along the walls at my dance studio.

"I went to an audition once before realizing what kind of dancer they wanted." I regretted my comment when her expression changed from pleading to annoyed.

She said, "Pole dancing is an art, and I need to be very good at it, if I want to earn enough tips to make a living." Her eyes lowered. "Without resorting to—"

I finished her sentence. "Lap dances."

"No, I need to give good lap dances, too, but no one will notice me if I suck at the pole." Her innocent young face showed no hint of irony over her word choice, or she set me up for her next comment. "I'm married and have a child. No way could I ever touch another man's penis and feel okay with myself."

I understood her limit, although she extended it a bit farther than my red line. The men in my past who assaulted me would not have settled for my fanny brushing across their laps, except maybe Kutash who got off on phone sex. Frankly, I couldn't understand the purpose of either male fetish other than foreplay before intercourse, my reason for establishing a solid redline.

"You want me to teach you something I've never done?" I reflected on my ice skating challenge back at *City Lites*. "I could watch you and make some suggestions, but, as you can see, I haven't installed a pole in this dance studio."

"I perform at a gentlemen's club, and they're always looking for new blood."

At age thirty-five, I hardly considered my blood new, but the idea started my old blood to warm up, tiger-like.

She added an incentive. "I'll give you half my tips, if you come and watch me."

What might that share amount to? Forty or fifty dollars? I sweated a full day on a movie set for not much more.

With her daughter in hand, she said, "Come any weekend after ten. I'll be on stage." She chuckled and whispered. "Or, on someone's lap."

***

The guy watching the door at the gentlemen's club eyed me suspiciously when I explained, "I just came to watch a girl do her routine at the pole."

"Lady, this is a first class club. Get your training at some off-the-beat joint, and then you have to apply for a permit to work here."

"I'm here to instruct, not perform."

"All our girls are over twenty-one, and that g-string never comes off. The boss is real strict."

"I said, instructor, not an inspector."

He gave a snort and walked away.

I observed a young girl working the pole. Not sure of the proper terminology, *working* definitely described the effort she exerted at the cost of ease and grace. Open crotch shots were offered too freely. I would like to see more body twists, hair flicks, and karate kicks, with loops around the pole. Probably upside down leg splits, oozing down the pole and rolling into double sitting-splits, clawing my way across the floor. I had to remind myself that I came to instruct, not perform.

The bouncer guy returned with my friend by the arm. "See what this woman wants, but be quick. You're to go on in a minute or two."

We pretended we didn't know each other. Not agreeing on what night to show up, I was intrigued with her ability to act out her part in a spur-of-the-moment encounter. We talked and I observed her act at the pole, smoother than the other girl but room for improvement. When I made my suggestions, her jaw dropped.

The bouncer, suspecting something fishy, shuffled up and said, "Okay, Sister. You get a turn." At least he said Sister rather than Mom, but I took it as a threat to embarrass me into leaving.

My friend said, "Go on up there, Mikel."

The bouncer glanced around, but all the girls were preoccupied. "You two need to stop talking and one of you get up there, pronto." He ambled off.

"Please, Mikel. I need to see those moves you just described."

A couple of Jeff Kutash-types eyed the two of us in an expression of freaky anticipation. His image repulsed, than challenged me. Coming from an evening rehearsal, I wore a loose fitting silk blouse over leotards. *Jaime, take notice of the long legs you never spread.* Mel Tellis had called them *Legs for days*, when I danced in *Jubilee*. They were about to be back in business.

I strutted onto the stage, approaching the pole with caution like the cubes at *Wild Things*. I grabbed the pole and did a simple spin straddling it with my legs spread. I catapulted my body up and performed the moves I'd visualized earlier with the same confidence I approached ice-skating that first time. I had developed the basic skills and applied them to a different dance routine. I ignored the likely skin burns I would suffer.

As a finale, I oozed to the floor and glided on my knees Jaime-style toward the audience, tipped onto my back caressing my body, legs, and breasts. Winking at the audience, I became slightly aroused.

The crowd began to chant, "Take it off, take it off."

The bouncer guy cupped his hands and yelled. "You heard the crowd."

So much for having a special permit to work in this *first-class* club. I called back, "That's what I came to do," my impulsive response exposing a hidden truth.

I did a Gypsy Rose Lee slowly unbuttoning my top. If only I had been wearing long gloves to pull off one finger at a time. Shaking my blouse loose over my shoulders, I swished it across the baldheads of the faces beaming up to me. I did a showgirl cooch across stage, the silk fabric playing peek-a-boo with my pink bra. Bluebell dancers had been provocative without going topless.

The audience continued yelling, "Take it off." I might have unsnapped my bra, if I could do it gracefully yet keep my arms covering my breasts.

I tossed my blouse aside and gestured for my friend to join me. She ditched her guy—money still tucked in the band of her g-string—and did a fairly good strut onto the stage. On the second pole, she followed my lead, improving with each repetition. She took the lead. I observed her moves and paid attention for subtleties that would enhance. She stood back, daring me to follow. I imagined Gene Nelson sparring with Gail Davis in an Annie Oakley routine, "Anything You Can Do I Can Do Better".

Preparing to promenade off stage, I scooped up my blouse, "Take it off," chanting in the audience. I nuzzled my back against my companion. "Unsnap it."

She released the hooks and backed away maintaining a provocative pose. Holding my bra in place with silk twirling above my head like a feathered fan, I caught the eye of a man seated at a table second row from the stage. Even in the smoky, dimly lit room, I could see he was wildly handsome. I winked and he reacted.

I was pumped. With the straps of my bra swinging back and forth, I faked tossing my blouse to the audience, and then dropped it behind me. A few boos from the crowd. I released my bra and swung it over my head. That opened the wallets and produced bills of all denominations. My keen sense of timing kicked in. When the crowd's enthusiasm peaked, I tossed my bra aside and stood breasts forward and arms outstretched, as if a curtain were about to close. I held that pose while my friend gathered the money.

With gawkers on three sides of the stage and no curtain, I gathered my clothes and, as gracefully as possible, stepped down from the stage. It cheapened my act, like a magician forced to explain the trick he had just performed.

I felt a tinge of embarrassment when a flashing strobe highlighted a couple of familiar male faces I hadn't noticed earlier. Either they didn't recognize me, or they assumed I would be discreet and not report to their wives. One I remembered from my time at *Jubilee*. I figured the men had more to be ashamed of than I did.

"Guess who I saw last night at a strip joint," won't begin their conversation with wives and family at the breakfast table.

I slid my arm through the sleeves of my blouse and strolled over to the fellow who had reacted to my wink. His aroma overrode the smell of beer and stale cigarette smoke.

Buttoning the bottom three buttons, I said, "If I wanted to start a club like this one, I'd install a curtain to give the dancers some dignity at the end of the act."

"I'll look into that when I redo the next one."

Idle banter or not, I was impressed but held back any reaction.

"That was quite a show you put on. Obviously, your training hadn't been limited to just pole dancing."

"I was a *Jubilee* Showgirl." A lifetime ago. "Mikel." I offered him my hand. "I was younger then."

"I'm Scott Meiers, the guy who redesigns clubs like this one. I doubt I could sell the idea of a curtain. Have a seat."

I grinned. "Not on your lap?"

"That's not my thing." He shoved back a chair. "What prompted you to come here tonight?"

Such a handsome face, beautiful sparking blue eyes. I considered responding financial need, but decided fate brought me here to meet this man. I said, "My friend's daughter is a student in my dance class, and she asked me to suggest how she might improve." I shook my head in disbelief. "Don't know what possessed me to get up on stage."

I felt his gaze scan my breasts, but I resisted glancing down to notice if my nipples protruded through the silk fabric.

We talked for the next couple of hours. Friends and cousins of his nephew about to be married twisted his arm to host a bachelor party at the club Uncle Scott had a hand in refurbishing. As we talked, I realized how intelligent and accomplished he was, his good looks already apparent when I winked at him. Father of two daughters—beautiful girls according to the cousins—he was going through a divorce and possibly available. Most important, he approved of my reason for coming to the strip club. My impulsive decision to perform didn't faze him, even earned his approval.

He glanced at his watch and said, "Wait here for me. I'll be back in half-an-hour." He stood and gestured toward my friend. "Check out your student. She seems to be doing quite well."

"My student's mother…" Words wasted as he headed toward the door. If he just flipped me off, so be it. If he returns like he said, this relationship has promise.

My friend came over and handed me a wad of bills. "Over a hundred, your share of the tips like I promised."

My eyes bugged. At *Jubilee* I earned an extra fifty dollars for going topless all week, twenty-five for each breast. I could not begin to calculate per-boob income, if this were a steady job. One glance at the stragglers who failed to score a date at the nightclubs further discouraged me from considering a career change.

My naiveté was about to experience one more shock. A man who had passed in and out of the club since midnight, decked out in tasteful but expensive jewelry, approached. He could have been a producer about to offer us a job, or an IRS agent wanting to grab the government's share of our tips.

He faced me and said, "How'd you like to double that handful of bills?" I backed away. My friend did not.

"You don't know how much I got." She showed the fist of money, and coquettish lips curled and puckered.

With his eyes still fixed on me, he said. "I know it ain't five of these." He flashed hundred dollar bills. "One three-song lap dance."

I retreated to Scott's party of nephew and friends, and, at the risk of being rude, my eyes remained glued to the transaction in progress. To think I was offered a chance to spend an evening with George Peppard for free.

I heard, "If you're shy, we can go into the back room. I have a key." Wow! Scott told me he, too, had a key when I asked what goes on behind the closed door. He reached into his pocket. "Go check it out if you like."

I didn't want to know then, but as the night went on, I became curious.

"Shy?" My friend wafted her hands in a welcoming gesture. "What makes you think I'm shy?"

She shoved him down onto the chair, put her hand on his bald-head as if it were a Barre at my dance studio and raised her leg to the left side of the chair imitating moves she had practiced on stage. With his nose bellybutton-high, she slowly unbuttoned her smock from the top down. He reached and she modestly brushed his hands away. She slid her arms free and swished the silky garment across his face creating a rasping sound against his five-o'clock-shadow, actually two-in-the-morning-shadow, playing peek-a-boo with her breasts brushing across his face. She began to gyrate.

The third song had hardly begun when he said, "You can stop now. I had enough." Still straddling his lap, my friend straightened and held a you-know-what-comes-next pose. He fanned a stack of hundred dollar bills at her and peeled off five.

He glanced my way. "You're almost as good as I'd hoped for," and he handed her a sixth bill. His gazed remained focused on me. "We want to see you and your friend around more often."

Scott had walked in and startled me. In defense of my gawking, I said, "My student just cleared a month's income at my studio. What are the chances of my being here when a fellow with that kind of money shows up?"

"Quite good. Almost any night when the crowd dies down. He oversees this club." He misread my stunned expression. "I hope you don't think my leaving was a pre-arranged cue for him to approach you."

"He knew who he wanted," I lied. I was pleased that he had chosen me, but proud to stick with my red line. However, I didn't let Scott off the hook. "It did seem strange, you walking out and telling me to stay."

"I went to my house to get the money I owed for your time tonight."

"My time? I don't work here or ever intend to."

"At least tonight, you wasted the follow-up action your dance generated. Anyone watching either had his lap dance or left the club, and the new crowd had no idea how good you were. This should cover your time spent with me." He handed me a balled up couple hundred dollars.

Two months later, we were living together, and I was pregnant.

 CHAPTER 30

Why the headlong rush into another relationship, especially after three that failed since Vince? I often asked that question about my personal choices; thankfully, most of my decisions supported the top-of-the-world phenomenon that never abandoned me.

Like my father but different from my mother, I was never meant to live alone, without a lover. Dad never gave up on intimate relationships, but Mom always kept some distance from Jim Mesnard, never fully opening her heart to him. I do not want her kind of loneliness when I am old. Mom had a full and wonderful life, and, as she reflects on it through her fog of dementia, I am sure she feels fulfilled. I want more.

In the back of my mind, I harbored the desire for a second child, but none of the men I dated felt right as a father figure for Nicholas or as a prospective parent of a child we would share. All were compatible socially, especially the three I allowed into my life intimately, but none was the family-type man I sought. Perhaps, I tried too hard to please my family more than myself.

Already when Nicholas was a toddler, Mom began to divide her time between living in Albuquerque and at my condo in Las Vegas, great for the three of us, but uncomfortable for an outsider to blend in. I won't say Mom interfered with any of my relationships, but she occasionally recognized some character flaws like alcohol and potential physical abuse. A mother can spot things that Gemini overlooks.

My mother's screening my male companions for her daughter's heart and womb often weighted my decision to give up and move on. One exception was Mike Milke. If I had loved him as much as she did, we might still be a couple. I enjoyed our time together. After Mom and Nicholas went to bed, we would spend hours at the pool sharing our dreams, he in athletics and teaching and I in performing and teaching dance. We both loved kids, and his students respected him. He earned a high student rating on the school-to-parent network.

Our relationship suffered when family related matters demanded my attention. In 1996, I relocated to my three-bedroom home that Mom helped me purchase but refused to move in with me. After a year of negotiations, Mom and Jim agreed to resettle separately in Vegas creating a flurry of activities, mostly involving Caroline and me.

When the dust settled, Mom innocently asked, "Whatever happened between you and Mike?" as if she had stepped aside to make room for him.

Not desperate, but certainly eager, I looked for a soul mate to help fill the three bedrooms in my new house, still not quite my dream home. Two short-term relationships later, I realized that neither was right for my son or for me. The first man turned out to be an ego covered with tattoos—my eight-year-old son called him *Karl, the tattoo man*.

The second guy, a greater misjudgment than the first. More jealous than David back at *Jubilee* who keyed my car, this guy rampaged through my home threatening me when I tried to break off the relationship. I called the police and he tore the cord from the wall. He had me pinned at the top of the stairs when the cops yelled for him to back off. He lunged toward them. With their weapons raised, he was lucky to come through it alive. Their restraining order worked for a while.

I decided to concentrate on my career, continue to raise my son, and pay attention to those episodes of my life that had been successful. If a relationship was to be in my future, so be it—I gave up searching.

Then Scott arrived. All indicators said *go*, not the least of which was the overwhelming sensation of our shadowy first meeting at the gentlemen's club. It was a replay of Richard Gere and Julia Roberts in *Pretty Woman*. My decisions are often impulsive but seldom romantic, until that moment. What do we tell our kids? That we met in a café? Of course, until they became adults and have already come to terms with their various parenting arrangements. It is the other people in my past who may find my honesty embarrassing or annoying who concern me.

At our parting that night we met, Scott said, "Tomorrow evening I'm handing out Halloween candy at my house. Stop by and meet my two daughters."

Was this to be our first date? Would his estranged wife also be there? It didn't feel comfortable, so I *stood him up*, or that's how he described my behavior when he called the next day. He felt hurt, and I learned how sensitive he was, a characteristic I hadn't found in a man since Douglas Nelson. I soon discovered Scott was also as generous. With Doug, I had been too immature to appreciate those qualities, but I learned to crave them. By way of an apology, I invited Scott to my house for afternoon coffee.

Without looking up from his cup, he asked, "What are your household expenses? I know living here can't be cheap."

The boldness of his comment startled me into a loss for words.

"I am offering half your expenses up to—"

"Hold on. I'm to be a *kept* woman?"

215

"I don't want you to go back to that club, ever again."

He understood my temptation but not my determination. "I'm not planning to go back." I needed to clarify my situation. "I never intentionally went there in the first place so how could I go back?"

"I know, but once you experience the taste of easy income, all highfalutin values go by the wayside when money problems get desperate."

"Are you asking to live with me?"

He hesitated, probably not prepared for such a blunt comeback to his forwardness. "Yes, but the financial offer still holds regardless."

"Pack your bags. You're moving in."

Silence. We made a life changing decision that needed quiet time.

"Mom, I'm home."

In life, timing is everything. "We're in the kitchen, Honey."

"Grandma picked me up at school."

"Say hello to my friend, Mr. Meiers." Scott, my son Nicholas Bryce Peterson."

Appearing caught off guard, Scott reached out as if unsure to shake hands or to ruffle my son's hair. "I'm pleased to meet you, young man."

Nicholas accepted his hand. "You coming to my football game?"

Scott chuckled. "If that's my invitation, I wouldn't miss it for anything."

"Mom, can Mr...?" He glanced from Scott to me. "Can your friend come with us tonight?"

"Of course, Honey. Now go find your uniform."

"Mikel! Nicholas and my daughter, Samantha, did a commercial together for the MGM Grand Adventures Theme Park.

An image Nicholas' dance partner emerged. "Wow! That's a coincidence."

216

"I brought her to practice one time when her mother was busy. I don't remember seeing you there."

"Nicholas doesn't like me standing over him, so I blend into the crowd to sneak a peek. However, I've talked to Samantha's mother. She reminded me of Doris Day."

Scott scowled and I nearly apologized for the comparison, or that she and I might have exchanged secrets. I merely wanted him to know we'd met.

His expression brightened. "Let's not tell our kids that we know. Their surprise will be fun."

I appreciated the chance to ease Nicholas into a new family setting. "It'll be like opening presents on Christmas morning." Scott will be a wonderful father to my son.

Throughout Nicholas' game that evening, I appreciated Scott's cheering my son on, but some buried negative reactions to the kids' commercial surfaced. I resented the new children-friendly theme replacing the earlier glamour of a showgirl culture.

Nicholas scored a touchdown, and Scott and I jumped up in unison. I returned to my new set of priorities, ever thankful for having been a part of the earlier glamour. I felt justified when the campaign failed, and MGM converted their Adventure Land into expensive high-rise apartments. Unfortunately, Kenny Rogers ditched his chicken franchise.

When Scott introduced his children to Nicholas and me, Samantha, his ten-year-old daughter, shouted, "Nick," as they clasped hands breaking into a well-rehearsed dance.

Performing a dosey-doe, he yelled back, "Why didn't you tell me Sam was coming over?" They just bestowed each other with family nicknames that stuck. Shallan, Scott's teenaged daughter, kept her composure but admitted the coincidence was remarkable.

Scott never questioned my past partners, even the guy who lurked in the ally across the street from our house. When he laid bouquets of flowers on the hood of my car, Scott reacted.

After an encounter out on the street with him, Scott came back into the house and commented in his usual soft tones. "I convinced your old boyfriend that hanging around here was a very, very bad idea."

His persuasive techniques exceeded that of law enforcement. If not the police, I never asked who or what convinced a violent stalker to leave me alone. Scott's presence in our lives became a cozy refuge from a cold, frightening world. I had never before felt so safe, or so forgiven.

Scott's recent past as a respectable husband and family man presented problems quite different from my being stalked by a jilted lover, and it required different persuasion. Jeannie, Scott's ex, had to call my number to reach him, and she recognized my voice from our sharing personal information during the MGM commercial. I realized that my situation as a former showgirl taking on menial jobs to survive suggested ulterior reasons for my entering into this relationship. My only selfish motive was my desire to fill an emotional void in my life. Financially, I maintained on my own while supporting my son and propping up my dance studio through some difficult times.

Our extended families slowly found common ground and settled into a somewhat comfortable relationship. Jeannie brought Samantha and Shallan over to see their dad but stayed in the car. I rushed out and invited her to join us. We began an extended family ritual of backyard barbeques at my house.

"He looks just like Clark Gable." Mom's fascination with movie stars paved the way for Scott to win her Good Housekeeping Seal of Approval. Not since I brought Douglas Nelson to Albuquerque as my fiancé to be baptized into our faith had she so overwhelmingly approved of my choice of mate.

Of course, Scott would give her a grandchild with his family name legally attached. She often complained that I hadn't removed Vince's name from Nick's birth certificate, or that I bestowed that honor on him in the first place. She had removed Caroline's and my father's name, *Chavez*, and replaced it with *Peterson* to match the rest of her children.

Scott and I didn't deny that we were a couple, and our relationship became obvious after I became pregnant.

CHAPTER 31

Scott's divorce had not been finalized, so he couldn't ask to marry me. We never felt our relationship needed a document to define what was in our hearts. A gift more precious than a diamond ring, he encouraged Nick to call him *Dad*, but only when my ten-year-old son felt ready. Scott wanted to earn that honor. He offered to adopt Nick, but we never got around to it like we never got around to getting married. I discouraged him from buying me expensive gifts to add to my collection of nice things. Sharing our lives together filled the void in my life that had developed from fleeting relationships.

He asked, "What I can do for you and Nick that would be something special?"

Not what can he buy, but what can he do for us. I loved it. My first reaction, a vacation at some romantic island, but I wanted our families to blend more than I needed a honeymoon.

"Mount Charleston." My inspiration created its own voice. It was close enough, so I wouldn't miss any dance classes. Spring recitals were a couple of months away, but my kids needed practice.

"Mount Charleston!" Scott shivered. "There's still a ton of snow up there."

"That's part of the plan. I want ice forts and snowball fights and you can build us a snowman."

"Well then, that's it."

"Only if you can talk your girls into going along."

"Sam wouldn't want to be left behind, but Shallan's probably too busy." He shook his head. "Tenth grade, and I'm sure you remember what that was like."

Boyfriends, sports, and dance. Scott's older daughter and I had a lot in common.

The rest of our merged families spent a weekend at the Resort on Mount Charleston, creating the *Peter-Meier-Son* fun brigade. After dinner Friday evening, Scott and I ordered drinks and gave Sam and Nick permission to explore the place.

By the time we returned to the room, the kids had torn the covers loose from both beds to make forts out of the sheets. They jumped from bed to bed, firing pillows at each other. Without a word, Scott and I grabbed the pillows from their hands as if about to scold. We exchanged glances and fired away. A few feathers continued to drift as two tired preteens took turns in the bathroom.

While Scott and I straightened the bedding, the image of Mom's king sized bed converted into a boxing ring popped into my head. Caroline and I would stand in our corners until Mom said, "Go." Our fights resembled kick boxing, because we did more jumping than making any physical contact, never any slugging. Exhausted, we would collapse onto the pillows. Sometimes, Caroline would doze off, but, as long as I can remember, I always preferred to sleep in my own bed.

I'm not sure if I became pregnant after the kids went to sleep that night, but earlier in the evening under the influence of music, candle light, and cocktails, we were primed to give it a whirl.

My second pregnancy had been planned full knowing who would take on the role of my child's father. Vince had accepted my son, but it wasn't like having my life-partner's baby growing in my body, a level of intimacy Vince and I never fully achieved.

Our weekend up on the mountain produced no snowmen or even snowball fights, but our families bonded. The living room at my house staged the *Nick and Sam Show*, sketches from *In Living Color* their most popular repertoire. Sam could curl her lips like Jamie Fox when he played Wanda. They entertained family and friends; Mom, Scott, and Mikel their main audience. We were on our way to becoming the *Brady Bunch*.

April fifth, midway into my pregnancy, Mom called with expected but sad news. "Jim passed away. Please call Caroline and tell her to come to Vegas."

I had talked to him earlier that week, promising to perform at his retirement home's spring celebration. Caroline and I would summarize the highlights of his life. We didn't prepare our presentation, but Caroline wrote a beautiful tribute that she read instead.

Mom refused to attend. "Those old people weren't his friends. We'll publish Caroline's obituary in the *Albuquerque Journal*."

Anticipating another grandchild kept Mom's spirits up, but Jim Mesnard's passing took its toll. Her only comment, "Too bad Jim didn't stick around long enough to see your baby," almost accusing him of running away. She never chastised him for his unhealthy life style; possibly kept an emotional distance to avoid the pain of losing him. They could have experienced a twenty-five-year intimate relationship.

No longer driving daily to sit with him, Mom parked her Honda Accord and refused to leave the house. The loss of her dear friend had affected her temperament. Living close by made it easy for me to stop and check if she was eating properly.

I brought her a Mexican dinner I had prepared, and she threw out onto the street. "I don't want this old Chimichanga." I refused to let the incident dampen our relationship. She was my mother and I loved her.

Scott stepped up his efforts to include her in our family activities. The crazy fun-loving *Peter-Meier-Son* family could take on any challenge, and we slowly lifted Mom from her funk.

On Sunday, September 13, 1998, André, my handsome boy, arrived nine months after the Mount Charleston affair. A natural kick boxer already before birth, his arms and legs relished in the newfound freedom outside my body. I had incubated a great athlete.

My son had graciously held off being born until a weekend, so I wouldn't miss any of my dance classes. On Friday, I told the kids there might be a substitute teacher when they returned. As predicted, on Monday a picture of baby André greeted them through the window and Jackie in leotards on the dance floor.

After pampering and powdering my beautiful baby from his bath, I realized I had an audience. Nick had the best view standing on a chair with his back pressed against his grandma and Scott at their side.

"He's your brother, Nick."

"I know, Grams. But he's so tiny."

He wiggled loose of my mother's grasp, jumped down, and ran off to other interests. She said, "André Duran Scott Meiers," as if calling her youngest grandchild to attention. "How did you ever come up with such a name?"

She had withheld suggestions/criticism about my bathing techniques, probably focusing all her concern about being left out of the naming process. I gave her my explanation, not for the first time, hopefully the last.

"I named him André after the tennis player, Agassi, Duran because he kicked and punched like an athlete, Scott because André was his first birth son, and Meiers to carry on the family name since his other children were girls."

Mom said, "I better see where Nick ran off to."

I carried Andre to my rocking chair and unbuttoned my blouse. Scott stood gazing at the wonderment.

I asked, "What do you think, an actor or an athlete?"

"Probably both, if he is anything like his brother." He lowered his gaze. "Just do whatever you and B.J. did with Nick. I'm not much good performing in front of an audience, and I'm certainly not the athletic type." He brightened. "At least not any more."

"You don't have to participate in sports, just give our boys opportunities and cheer them on." His ego needed a boost. "Surfboarding and water skiing like you taught Nick. Maybe add snow skiing."

Scott said, "André Duran Scott Meiers. When you turn ten, we're going to a San Diego Chargers game just like your mother and I did for Nick's tenth birthday."

Scott followed through with water related activities, but never tossed a ball or shot hoops with the boys. Mom and I took over until Andre excelled beyond our level of ability.

As a family, we boated on Lake Mead and surfed the Pacific Ocean beaches. Scott had been a surf bum since childhood on into his mid twenties, when an oncologist told him he was in danger of developing skin cancer. He would spend seven hours a day riding the waves when he wasn't at one of his many jobs to finance his education and later to establish a reputation in his drafting career.

Our family vacations gravitated to the coast, Laguna Beach, Newport Beach, and Balboa Beach offering the widest range of surf conditions for various experience levels. Scott taught his boys the three main types of waves; beach for novice surfers, reef for more predictable waves, and point that can produce epic waves. Waves that peak can break left and right, and it can be ridden in either direction. Scott stressed patience and caution, selecting the right wave but prepared for the one that could wipe you out.

He told the kids about the point wave that nearly drowned him and seven of his surfer buddies. He also told and retold about two Northridge earthquakes that made the ground wave like the ocean, and his Oklahoma grandfather who wore the barrel of his pistol thin on one side by drawing it from its holster so often.

On the beach, Scott taught the children to make sand sculptures of dolphins, sea horses, or anything they wanted. They cheered as the tide washed away their sand castles. I was proud of Scott's artistic talent and his effort to pass some of those skills on to his kids.

Not into ocean swimming, I cheered and developed tan lines, topless dancing only a memory. In winter, I joined my family racing down the ski slopes at Brian Head in Utah.

Weekends, we would pull our 20-foot Chaparral to the lake. Rather than buying a bat and ball like some fathers, he gave our infant son a life jacket with 101 Dalmatians design.

He said, "He'll grow into it."

He taught Nick and Sam to operate the boat, strictly enforcing the safety rules, and promised to do the same for their brother.

André and Nick began life in my body ten years apart, but I need to reflect on their formative years in parallel. Being first to emerge from the womb is not an entitlement like some European dynasty.

Their fathers are strong handsome men, both artistic right-brain dominant, but I put more trust in their zodiac signs than brain theory. Nick's birth date lies on the borderline between a Libra and a Scorpio. Bits of each description fit his personality; extremely sociable, loves to communicate, seldom at a loss for words. A natural leader, his friends look to him to organize their activities. When it suits him, he can produce Scorpio's sting.

Virgo somewhat defines Andre's personality, denying feelings and pretending everything is okay even when it's not. Unfortunately, he has a tinge of that zodiac sign's unpredictable and sometimes testy temperament. What Virgo failed to identify was André's charm and likeability. And, the athlete he has become.

These factors were out of my control. As their mother, I strove to create a favorable environment from conception. During my pregnancies, I kept healthy physically and emotionally, but not all external influences can be controlled by eating and exercising. With Nick, I had to go it alone, and I was strong enough to thrive and survive. Scott and I approached my pregnancy with André as a team. From a family point of view, my sons' early childhoods were quite similar, a stable two-parent home life with a goal oriented mother for herself and her boys.

Both my pregnancies occurred at crazy periods in my life, as if there ever had been a time when I wasn't hyperactive active. With Nick, coming off a high from three years in *Jubilee* and the '88 Pre-Olympics in Korea, I had to adjust to a new relationship with Vince in an unfamiliar city, as well as dealing with a first pregnancy. With André, adjusting to a more complicated family relationship was my only challenge. I was older, wiser (smarter but still impulsive) and better prepared for the onslaught of parenting.

André's mom had settled into a routine, whereas Nicholas experienced a glamorous Mikel interacting with celebrities until a midlife crisis—showgirls reach this point sooner than most of the population. In my case, it occurred in stages between my *Siegfried and Roy* experience and the demolition of the Dunes Hotel. However, I was able to shelter Nicholas emotionally from each of these setbacks. I'm not so confident that my three short-term relationships between Vince and Scott didn't affect my son in a negative way. However, Scott and I created a stable home life for Nick from age ten on.

A major childhood difference, Nick had been an only child and André came into a three generational family; two parents, a brother, two half-sisters who lived close by with their mother, and Grams right around the corner.

As the youngest of four siblings, André received a lot of attention. Sam and Nick treated him as a little tag-a-long monkey named *Dré*, Shallan's abbreviation of *André*. Kelli Crossley, my dance student and her mom, Lisa, helped me organize the Baby America Pageant in Las Vegas. I had choreographed Kelli and Nick as dance partners for recitals and auditions.

At the Las Vegas pageant, André won and went on to Universal Studios Pageant in California. He, of course, won over-all baby awards, most photogenic, costume, personality, cutest baby, and on-and-on. He took it all home, crown, cape and scepter, two six-foot tall trophies, ten medium trophies, and cash and bonds set aside for lessons in dance and karate.

Crowned Miss Teen Nevada in 2005, Kelli has since moved out to Los Angeles booking many roles in films and commercials. Feb 16, 2009 she scored her first musical hit, "Hostage." I am very proud of her and thankful of our time together.

CHAPTER 32

One morning, a late-model red pickup sat outside the front door to my studio with a man sound asleep at the wheel. His face seemed familiar from some show or performance, but I couldn't quite place it. Many black entertainers had found opportunities in Las Vegas since Sammy Davis Jr. and others blazed a trail. Not sure if he was possibly dead, I cautiously approached the open window.

"Hello?"

Startled awake, he apologized profusely and tried to explain his situation. "I noticed your studio sign and waited until you opened...must have fallen asleep."

"You look familiar. Were you by chance on the Jerry Lewis telethon?"

"Yes ma'am. Did that show ten years ago." He stifled a yawn, but his eyes glistened. Still trying to put a name to his face, he misread my inquisitive expression. "I'm not some homeless vagabond. I just drove up from LA, hoping to find a studio to practice my tap." He reached across the steering wheel and extended his hand through the window. "Excuse my manners. My name is Lindell Blake."

"Lindell Blake? Not *the* Lindell Blake?"

"I'm the only one I know of."

"I'm thinking of the video *Smooth Criminal*. You aren't *that* Lindell Blake."

"I sure am. Danced with Michael Jackson. I'm the guy." He released my hand and gazed down at the steering wheel. "I'm afraid I lied about not being homeless."

"And you haven't had breakfast." I grinned. "And don't lie about that, too."

"I've got cash enough for food and gas. Just need a dance floor to hone my skills and a restroom to freshen up." He glanced at the crumpled blanket on the passenger side. "I expect to sleep in my truck until I get that job and a paycheck."

"Let's start with breakfast, and then we can talk about a job." He seemed to squirm. "Come on in. You can use the bathroom, while I get the studio ready for class."

I checked out the area from last evening's ballroom dance class and prepared it for the morning jazzercise group, both I had sub-let to other instructors. Out emptying the trash, I heard the clicking and clattering of steel toes on wood. Back inside stood an amazed jazzercise instructor and a few adult students agog at Lindell's routine. His need to break into a dance far exceeded his need for food.

I waited for a slight pause and applauded him, a signal that he should stop to allow the jazzercise class to begin.

"Don't stop him!" A unison voice from everyone clustered around Lindell Blake. He continued another ten minutes before he even realized people had gathered.

"I'm sorry. I didn't mean to intrude."

The crowd, after a moment of stunned silence and dropped jaws, broke into a vigorous applause. Lindell tapped his way to the bench, took off his performance shoes, and exchanged them with sneakers from his cloth bag. Already that morning, I felt a second job offer in the wind for Lindell.

Over bagels and coffee, we compared our experiences with Kenneth Feld productions, Lindell's at *Madhattan* in 1998 and mine with *Siegfried and Roy* almost a decade earlier. I told him about my neighbor, Willie, who performed at *Ringling Brothers and Barnum Bailey Circus* back in the thirties, another Feld production. At age 14, Lindell danced in *Swing, Swing, Swing,* at the Sands two years before the hotel closed in 1996, about the same time I established *Mikel's Performing Arts Academy.* Moving between New York, California, and Las Vegas, his most recent Vegas performance was an early version of his *Spoken Word, Spoken Feet* in *Madhattan* at the New York, New York, followed by a couple of barren years.

With all that success, he did not deserve to be destitute, but so it goes with the world of entertainment. I recalled my desperate need to win the turkey back in grade school and a few times since when the only thing between poverty and me was my next dance job. I felt pleased to help Lindell get back on his feet.

Another concern we shared was our mothers' wellbeing, his originally from Trinidad and couldn't stand the cold climate of New York. Lindell planned to bring her to Vegas when he settled, and Betty Jeanne had already moved here a few years earlier.

By time we got back from breakfast, the jazzercise class had ended and the studio was dark. Lindell hesitated to get out of my car. "You don't suppose I could use the floor until your next class?"

"It's all yours. Just don't let anyone in while I'm gone."

When I returned with Nick from school, a few people had gathered outside the front window peering in.

"What's going on, Mom?"

"It's the surprise I promised. Go check it out."

Didn't take my son long to work his way to the front of the on-lookers. Moments later, Lindell took a break and all but Nick walked away, his face still buried in hands cupped against the glass.

I said, "That's Lindell Blake from *Smooth Criminal.*"

Nick shouted, "He's the guy who busted the pool cue."

"Let's go in and meet him." Nick had studied Michael Jackson's moves in *Smooth Criminal* for one of his stage performances. He approached Lindell imitating Michael Jackson and stammered, "Hi."

I had never seen him at a loss for chatter. "Lindell, this is my son, Nick."

"Hi, back at you, Nick." Lindell held out his hand, manicured fingers curved down.

Touching knuckles loosened my son's tongue. "I can do Michael Jackson." Nick, whose birth coincided with the release of *Smooth Criminal* over a decade earlier, faced the veteran actor and demonstrated more of Jackson's bravado.

Lindell responded with some counter moves. "Hey, you're pretty good."

"Was that a real pool cue? Did it hurt your leg when you broke it?"

"Yes, it was the real thing, but the prop manager had already pre-broken it and stuck it back together."

Nick nodded. "I kind of guessed it was a trick."

"We had to re-do that scene a dozen times. That would be a lot of cue sticks to destroy."

"And a hurting leg." My son bantering with Lindell Blake! I was so proud.

As the kids arrived that afternoon, I asked their parents if they would enjoy learning to tap dance. Some had danced professionally, and most of the others were closet-dancers when alone in the house. Enough signed up to offer Lindell a teaching job.

At our first class, I demonstrated my Broadway style tapping, arms swinging and body swaying. The normally polite and demure Lindell Blake busted out laughing. Rather than be offended, I stepped up the action, until I doubled up giggling and gasping for air.

Lindell promoted a balance between the body-erect Michael Flatly style and Gregory Hines' bend at the hips backward-forward action, feet a blur in each. He objected to Flatly's rigid and prescribed dance patterns. Some of Lindell's improvising included doing the splits and slowly elevating himself vertical without using his hands and doing back flips in the middle of a tapping sequence.

I recommended Lindell to a couple of my agents for additional dance jobs in the area, and he hit the pavement looking for work.

When Nick objected to having his mother in the same class, Scott said, "Hire Lindell for private lessons. We'll find the money someplace."

My son and Lindell Blake, developed routines and performed them at recitals, their most successful at Palo Verde High School.

Our family became good friends with Lindell, even two-year-old André who was well on his way to becoming a star in his own right. I gave Lindell a key to my studio for practice, and I offered him the use of our guest bedroom for a couple of months until he could afford an apartment. Lindell brought excitement and rhythm to our home. Soon Nick and André developed a beat in their step. The pattern spilled over to Scott and me, slicing carrots, sweeping the floor, doing dishes had to be performed to a count. Beating eggs and whipping cream were especially creative and sometimes messy.

Sam and Nick invited friends over to meet Lindell, and he graciously participated in their impromptu skits to entertain Mom, Scott and me. Add an occasional neighbor, and our family room felt crowded. I kept my dream-house in the back of my mind, but not to happen for another three or four years.

Once Lindell regained his stride, he did some of his best work in Las Vegas. He landed a dance job in *Midnight Fantasy* at the Luxor where he addressed the packed auditorium. "This number is for my friends, Mikel and Scott Meiers." We were ecstatic.

In his one-man show, *Spoken Word, Spoken Feet*, Lindell developed five different characters who related their stories through dance. In addition to commercial success, *An Afternoon with Lindell Blake*, his three part recital series at the West Las Vegas Art Center in spring of 2012, grounded him in the arts.

He ultimately moved his mother to Vegas, but she and my mother never met.

CHAPTER 33

"André? André!"

I scooted up the aisle and back down, checking each direction. "No," I whispered, trying to slow my racing heart. He hasn't been abducted, just playfully hiding.

"Where's André?" I shaded my eyes scouting away from of the rack of boys' outfits where I expected to hear his giggle. "Where's André?"

I needed to tease further. At five, he'd developed some restraint at giving away his hiding places. "Well, if André ran away, I'll just pick out his shirt without him." I began parting hangers from the opposite end of the rack where I expected to find him pressed between the clothes.

My heart rate increased. He would have screamed bloody murder if anyone tried to abduct him. I taught him that. Such a handsome boy needed extra caution.

"I lost my son," I said loud enough for him to hear and to get the attention of a passing sales clerk.

A chuckle in her voice, she said, "I'm too busy to look for a lost child right now. I have to undress this boy-mannequin and give it new clothes." She blocked my view of her intended target. "Now, who put these two display pieces side-by-side? I'll just move one back where it belongs."

"No! I want to stay here with my friend." André's voice as the live mannequin pulled his arm tighter around the neck of the plastic one, both cheerfully smiling. His studying the mimes at St. Mark's Square in the Venetian Hotel had its effect; surprising he didn't hold out his cap for tips.

"I'll talk to the manager and see if I can get your son a job as a human display in the boys' department," the sales person joked.

"He'd never last a minute without an energy burst." Already surpassing my prediction, I stepped into view of André's profile just as he winked at a girl about his age. She stopped and stared, her mother obviously annoyed at her daughter's dallying.

André finger-waved and said, "Hi."

Astounded, the girl muttered back, "Hi," and her mother burst out laughing. Half-a-dozen shoppers stopped and stared before my son tired of his game.

André, our little entertainer. Always doing silly things like climbing up to the top of his bunk bed and hiding among his stuffed animals, his little face in a freeze-pose pretending to be one of them. It reminded me of Nick hiding in the dresser drawer under Vince's clothes. Scott feeding André spaghetti was a repeat of Vince and Nick, boys scooping hands-full of noodles and sauce all over their faces.

Time for number two son to make his debut at *Mikel's Performing Arts Academy*. He had been resting on his laurels and on his cuteness since Baby America Pageant, and he needed to be productive, not just playing soccer, karate, and t ball. In an Eskimo costume, brownish fur covering his pant legs and a hood nearly burying his face in fluff, André led a single file of dancers onto the stage. He turned to begin his routine with his partner, but she panicked and ran away.

236

"Go back and keep dancing." My stage-whispered response to any disruption stopped him in his tracks. Like a baseball runner caught between third base and home plate, he took steps in both directions. Giving up, he stared at the remaining dancers doing their sequence without him.

I gently aimed his partner back toward him and said, "André is waiting for you, sweetheart." Her courage restored, she joined him in their routine. Sometimes, accidental goof-ups are the funniest.

Hips swaying and guitar twanging, with eyes hidden behind Hollywood shades, hair slicked, and sideburns to his chin, André, in a tropical colored shirt, white pants, and jacket with a silver sequined collar, did his Hawaiian number. Five years after his debut at Baby America Pageant, André's Elvis had returned.

In another tropical number, Scott and a couple other fathers had built a portable staircase where kids dressed as fruit posed while being pushed onto the stage. On the bottom level stood a girl in a grape-cluster costume, on up the stairs sat a human strawberry, an apple, a pineapple, all the way to my son, the *Top Banana*. Older dancers took each child's hand and helped them down the steps to dance their routine, reminiscent of human dice in *Cabaret Circus* at the Lady Luck Hotel and Casino.

Charlie Chaplin with a triangular moustache, vest jacket, and bowler hat became André's signature character performing solo with his cane. In contrast, he appeared as Fonzie riding out on a toy electric motor cycle with training wheels wearing leather jacket, blue jeans, and sunglasses. Whenever André appeared, the stage turned electric.

Two other families joined my family to form the core support for *Mikel's Performing Arts Academy*. Desiree and Lynn with their children Brandon, Dustin, and Karli, and Brenda and Ron with their children Chad, Thomas, and Anthony were our barbeque-in-the-backyard type of neighbors. The parents built stage props, and Scott added artistic designs for themes from Broadway shows, Academy Awards, movies, the 50's, celebrity look-a-like, and a journey through time. Each recital became a production show.

We three families attended our kid's sporting events, went boating and picnicking together on weekends, and traveled as a group to perform at Knott's Berry Farm in California each year.

Brandon Hughes added the most drama to our household as well at on stage. Back at the condo—both our families moved into America West homes about the same time—as a child, he rode Nick's Big Wheels down the stairs, and his flare for gutsy adventure never diminished. He could have been cast as the kid from the movie *Home Alone*.

With André nestled in a bed sheet, Brandon and Chad began rocking the bundle back and forth like a hammock. It soon turned into a jumping rope making a complete swing, André catapulting out. A broken nose, our first family injury of note. Jim Mesnard, we need another Band Aid.

For the recital theme, *Movies and Motion Pictures*, a routine from *Dirty Dancing* required partnering and lifting the girls. Nick, Brandon, and Chad rounded up classmate volunteers, mostly football players. The event stimulated a couple budding romances. Eventually, Brandon married his partner, Breanne, and they are raising a family. Today, they are lifting and flipping pancakes as managers of the Cracked Egg restaurant on Ann Road. Scott really liked Breanne and had hoped she and Nick would date.

My mother encouraged both boys' interest in sports when they were toddlers, tossing a ball for them to catch or to swing at with a bat. There was no period in their young lives when she wasn't living with us at least six months out of each year, full time in her own house after 1996, and in our home after 2007.

She cheered her grandsons through little league t-ball to high school sports and, in Nick's case, throughout college. No doubt, she had the same hopes for my brother, Jeffery, only to have them dashed when he fell apart at the peak of his near professional baseball achievement.

With team sports, André followed Nick's footsteps from t-ball on to baseball, basketball, football, and lacrosse. They both excelled with roller blades, skateboards and surfboards, and continued dancing; hip-hop, tap, and some ballroom to enhance their athletic skills. I respected their rule, *don't ever try to put us in ballet*, but they accepted acting and modeling classes because those activities earned them parts in movies and commercials.

Garehime Grade School displayed my boys' trophies for athletic records set. At Centennial High School, Nick lettered in football, track, and lacrosse. André will likely earn a scholarship in football. *Fearless*, is how his coach described him as a wide receiver.

Nick developed his extensive résumé, through modeling and acting with emphasis on dance. His commercials included, Maryland Square, Kids Kamp, MGM Theme Park, Summerlin and Las Vegas CAT Bus Service. He earned small parts with me in the movies *Mars Attack*, 1996, and *Fools Rush In*, 1997, and he performed the stunts for a gang member in *Pay It Forward, 2000*, a movie that took place at Centennial High School from which he graduated a few years later.

He took on dance and modeling jobs at conventions such as Magic Jungle Rags, LA Sketchers, Obermeyer Sky Show, and Magic Warner Brothers. His repertoire of impersonations included Blues Brothers, Elvis, Austin Powers and George Michaels. He excelled in Karate, a dozen different sports, and as many dance styles, most of which he took home trophies from competition.

I insisted he put three quarters of his earnings in savings, and when he turned seventeen, he had a nice sized down payment on a pickup. I worried that he should save for college, but he solved that problem by earning a lacrosse scholarship at Notre Dame Demiur, Belmont, California.

Four years later, our family car jam packed with Scott and his daughters, André, Mom and me, about to set off for Nick's graduation when my cell phone rang.

"Mom, Dad, I need a special sash for my graduation gown. I've made the honor role."

The school supplied the gown, and Scott paid the bill. For a few precious months, Nick rejoined the *Peter-Meier-Son* household until he could he could find employment suitable for his business science and marketing degrees.

Shallan Meiers, Scott's older daughter, was a beautiful and talented young lady, modeling since age thirteen and earning the title *Little Miss Las Vegas* in 1999. Three years later, Hugh Heffner selected Shallan as Playboy-of-the-Month for the September 2002 issue. Heffner offered her the opportunity to be one of three traveling companions. Reporters suggested *Playboy's Miss September 2002*, had the perfect look to become one of the three finalists on the Fox special, *Girl Next Door.*

Shallan agreed to the first offer and rejected all others. I approved her decisions. Her red line had been tested, and it prevailed. When her mother decided not to attend any of the parties at the Heffner Mansion, I felt disappointed that Shallan hadn't asked me. At her age, I had an offer to appear in *Playboy Magazine* featured as a showgirl, but *Jubilee* rules would not allow it.

Shallan gave her dad a gift box of 25 Gran Corona cigars from Hugh Heffner. He smoked the cigars, and saved the signature wooden cigar box hand crafted by Don Diego.

Samantha moved to Arizona after graduation where she married and is raising a family.

***

I continued teaching and performing whenever agents could produce jobs, but much of my income went to support *Mikel's Performing Arts Academy*. When the landlord increased my rent, moving to another location, or worse, the demise of my program, appeared to be likely. Frustration—that helpless feeling from back stage when a student encounters a problem during a recital. One time, a little girl's laces came undone, and she spent her whole number tying her tap shoe. My stage whisper, "Keep dancing," from the sidelines only added to her confusion.

I drilled the concept into my students' reflexes. *Keep dancing.* If you lose a shoe. *Keep dancing barefoot.* If you fall down. *Get up and keep dancing.*

"What should you do if your friend falls?" My trick question in two different situations and my students learned to make the distinction. *On stage, keep dancing, any other time, stop and help your friend.* Dancers need to be competitive, but no shoving or put-downs, please. Insensitive and sometimes brutal behavior happens often enough, and dealing with it early-on is important. Those of my students who continued to dance professionally thanked me for insisting on manners and ethical behavior on stage and behind the curtains.

At all costs, Mikel, keep dancing. I applied my rule and refused to disappoint my students. In 2000, the Durango Hills Community Center, a new 51,000-square-foot facility operated by the YMCA in conjunction with the City of Las Vegas, offered me employment. Eventually, I performed seven separate job descriptions. I taught high impact aerobics, monitored their outdoor pool and inside exercise room, did minor maintenance chores, assisted after-school programs, and held birthday parties. On Sundays, I filled in as

241

building supervisor. When their aqua teacher gave notice of quitting, I observed her a few times and took over her class.

I noticed an exercise room remained unscheduled during the time I would be at *Mikel's Performing Arts Academy* teaching my kids. I approached Mike Lubbe, Southern Nevada YMCA president and CEO, with an offer of a fifty-fifty split of revenue, if I could bring my class to that room. The YMCA at Durango and later at Centennial was established as partnerships between the city and the YMCA, and my offer was an extension of that concept. Mike agreed with my argument and was happy to fill an unused room. He suggested a less encompassing title such as *Mikel's Dance Class*.

When the Durango Hills Golf Course opened, the manager hired me to run their mobile refreshment cart. Through charm and a genuine interest in people's lives, I generated as much as eight hundred dollars in sales each day during a good weekend. I also bartended for private parties, both minimum wage job with good potential for tips.

I had come full circle with my days at The Daisy in Beverly Hills.

CHAPTER 34

In Genesis 41:27, Joseph interpreted Pharaoh's two dreams as seven fat years followed by seven lean years. I took that to mean life consists of good and bad episodes, not always a predictable number. Yet, my fourteen-year relationship with Scott pretty well matched the Biblical example.

Mom's excitement after receiving a postcard advertising homes in Spanish Springs, an upscale housing development, met with little resistance from me. We went to check it out, and I put money down on one of the lots. André had started kindergarten that fall, freeing my day to earn more income. Scott's architectural design business fluctuated, but more-often-than-not, he had been able to maintain his commitment made at my kitchen table the day after Halloween six years earlier. He certainly accepted his parenting role with André and Nick.

I called Caroline that evening and suggested Cindy listen in. "Guess what Mom and I did today." I allowed my customary three-second pause to my *guess what* conversation openers. "We went to look at some new houses being built, and I bought one."

"Just one?" I usually appreciated Caroline's witty comments, but this one stung a little.

"I signed a contract contingent to selling my house." I increased my pause to five or six seconds. "Would you guys be interested in a good deal on my three-bedroom house?" An audible gasp, not sure if from Caroline or Cindy. "No realtor costs involved," I added to sweeten the pie.

I spewed out some figures the agent had worked up. Caroline gave her usual lecture about making rash decisions, so I brought our mother back into the discussion. "I think Mom had her eye on the ground-floor bedroom and bath off the family room, in addition to kitchen, dining and family rooms." Caroline and I agreed Mom would never have to go to an *old folk's home*, her idea of a senior care facility like where Jim Mesnard spent the end of his life.

A long pause I knew better than to interrupt. She said, "Get a couple of appraisals and we'll talk."

To my surprise, they called back with an offer to buy both my properties, but I needed the condominium rental income to apply to my house payments. With the equity from my three-bedroom house, I was able to put down twenty percent of the purchase price to secure a low interest loan. As with most everything in my life, I charged ahead into uncharted waters, the end result still unknown. However, the equity will supplement my retirement. Entertainers aren't offered job security let alone savings plans.

What about Scott? Everything happened so fast, he didn't have time to digest the news. As I expected, he gave a nonchalant approval, as if he hadn't expected to be part of the decision or he understood what my dream home meant to me. He had designed custom home conversions in Del Webb's Gold Key Program at Sun City Summerlin, and he approved the floor plan I'd chosen without suggesting alterations. He appreciated having an office.

I am proud of what I accomplished, but property never dictated my life. Whether a coincidence or just one of separate issues, the new house marked the beginning of a curtain that slowly dropped between Scott and me. Each of the three homes I bought put pressure on my relationship at the time, Vince with my condo, possibly Mike Milke with my three bedroom purchase, and now Scott. I sloughed off the notion, but Scott's attitude toward intimacy took a dip. He hadn't taken a lover, because they would have had to meet in our kitchen where he did his design work, his office depressed him.

Attention once lavished on me, Scott redirected to fewer design projects. With Del Webb's Summerlin development completed, he covered Rhodes Ranch in a similar capacity. Rezoning in 2002 to curb strip clubs ended his string of contracts redesigning gentlemen's clubs. From then on, jobs came by way of reputation and word of mouth. He struggled to maintain steady work, and intimacy between us continued to slacken. By the collapse of the housing market in 2007, we were sleeping apart, but in the same king-sized bed.

The white knight who rescued me a decade back had fallen into careless personal habits, his lack of concern for our relationship turned on himself, heavy smoking, slovenly dressed, poor diet, and lack of exercise. A compulsive workaholic all his life intensified, but on fewer and fewer projects, always striving for perfection. He rejected the trend for computer generated cookie-cutter techniques; the artist in him demanded his projects reflect a human hand. He wasn't a structural architect but an architectural design consultant. His promises of grandiose schemes never materialized.

My sister Caroline, the only person I felt comfortable sharing my feelings—Mom idealized Scott and no way would I put a wedge in their relationship—suggested counseling. I couldn't destroy what little pride he had left to prop up his faltering ego. He had been my rock, and now that foundation began to crumble. I considered seeking help through the church, but the minister made it quite clear that I was operating outside his fold, living in sin according to his sermon the very next Sunday after meeting Scott. He either tolerated my previous *boyfriends* or was not aware of them or considered them temporary and forgivable.

Life's trials had toughened me, no longer needing to be coddled. So I thought. I could make this relationship work and take care of our boys. Scott's love and attention to them remained constant, but tending to their physical needs became my assigned duty. I hadn't considered separating, because André should experience family life that Nick had missed when Vince and I parted. I took on more financial responsibility and household obligations freeing Scott to earn whatever he could after the whole economy went south. We had become two strangers with common goals. For the last seven years of our relationship, we had not enjoyed any intimacy.

During that time, Nick graduated from high school and college with honors. André completed elementary grades and was doing well in middle school. I focused on what was left of my career, dance lessons and exercise classes, and experimented with other opportunities. At the YMCA and Durango Hills Golf Course, I accepted every opportunity to earn money, with reasonable success.

Tired, I let my guard down. The quickness with which it happened during the YMCA basketball tournament didn't allow time for reflection. Supervising the building on weekends had been my responsibility, and when we hosted the basketball tournament, my hours extended from morning to late at night. Although problems of crowd control or safety seemed remote, my manager hired a security person, and coaches used him to run errands. Each time someone needed something from another part of the building, I would have to open locked doors and take note of what was borrowed to be sure it went back in its proper place. Passing through hallways and into storage areas, we talked and shared bits of our lives.

Charles, nickname Corky, definitely met my criteria for attractive, strong, intelligent men, but none ever interfered with my existing relationship. Until Corky. Our shared interests included taste in music, athletic working out and training, operating a small business, and a curiosity about the functioning of mechanical things. We each capitalized on our skills, he hired out as a coach and a personal trainer, and I doing private investigation work at the Casinos.

I shared some of my recent PI experiences on the Strip tracking down and taking pictures of cheating husbands, serving legal papers, and looking out for hooker/bartender collusion. His eyes lit up with genuine interest, something no one else found as fascinating.

As football captain at Indiana State University, he led his team to the 1A National Championship in 1983. He made it as far as NFL camp where a previous injury blew a possible professional career. A former All American Wrestler in high school, he trained and coached the sport at Bishop Gorman High School for eight years and at Faith Lutheran High School for three years. He and his ex-girlfriend built and operated a *Biggest Loser House* with the most success of other weight loss programs in Vegas homes. As a fallback career, he is a master electrician. He has four beautiful daughters.

At closing the night of the second and last weekend, Corky jotted his phone number on a slip of paper, pressed it into my palm, and scrunched my fingers around it.

The simple touching of hands sent a jolt of electricity through my body. I stared at my fist dumbfounded. The boundaries that allowed our sharing of personal issues over the past two weeks evaporated.

He said, "You're not going to call, are you?"

I handed the paper back.

His blue eyes penetrated. "Let's set a date right now for next Tuesday."

I stared blankly, and slowly shook my head.

"Tonight, then. Let's go to Timber Lodge for a drink to celebrate a successful tournament."

"That will be after ten." I should have said "No."

"I'll wait."

"Not tonight. I have to get home." What am I saying? Why didn't I just say goodbye and leave?

He stood and stared, finally breaking the silence. "I'll call you."

"No." A man calling me at my home would violate everything family represented. A part of me didn't want to send him away. "I'll meet you next Friday after my dance class. We can have an early dinner. Just something simple."

"Okay. I'll stick around until you lock down the place tonight."

"That would be nice." I am a very self-reliant person, but I've experienced too many scary moments, especially in parking lots after dark.

Lights out, alarm set, and doors locked, Corky's pickup idled out front with headlights aimed toward my car. Seated with my door shut, he pulled up alongside.

"Friday, see you."

I was so flustered, I nearly called out, "Where?" I remembered Timber Lodge. He had stopped there each morning of the tournament to pick up breakfast and coffee for us. On the drive home, I rationalized how innocent my meeting a friend after dance class would be. We enjoyed each others' company, and following up on our friendship would be normal. Deep down, I knew it would spark something serious between us. Most sadly, Scott and my boys might not believe I had remained faithful during those painful years of deprived intimacy.

 CHAPTER 35

I began a difficult but necessary conversation with Scott in our back yard. "I'm seeing someone."

"Seeing? Don't you mean sleeping with?"

"Just seeing." My gaze settled on the rusted barbeque grill. "For now."

"Like we were *just seeing* each other after meeting at a strip joint."

"Gentlemen's club," I corrected. "We were free to act on our feelings back then. Now, there are consequences."

"Are you and mystery man prepared to accept those *consequences*? Even aware of what they might be?"

"Yes, I am." I held eye contact. "Our sons' anger, and," I lowered my gaze. "And, your hurt feelings." I drew a deep breath. "Believe me, this has not been an easy decision, or I would have made it half-a-dozen years ago when we drifted apart." I considered *fell out of love* but realized we continued to love and respect each other, especially as parents.

"And, I'm not entitled to get angry?"

"We both knew this moment was bound to happen. Our sons didn't."

"André?"

Silence, neither of us able to find the right words.

"Fine!" Scott stormed into the house.

I glanced skyward for spiritual support but felt a wave of guilt. I immediately lowered my eyes. The cover to the barbeque grill hanging by a single hinge matched the image of our broken relationship.

God, don't give up on Your daughter. I need you now more than ever.

I headed into the house to explain how I felt. Seeing Scott hunched over his drawings at the kitchen table—he no longer used his office to work—I realized no explanation would be satisfactory. Whatever the situation was, he needed to be left alone.

Had I continued our relationship another five years until André left for college, my resentment of Scott's lack of interest would have grown. I would have blamed Scott for my unhappiness.

Our commitment hadn't an exit clause like back with *Splash* at the Riviera when I wanted to quit and join *Siegfried and Roy*. The social contract between Scott and me bound us tighter than a marriage certificate with implied divorce options. No ritual or ceremony defined the beginning of our relationship with no endgame strategy. As a result, we continued living independent lives long before any decision to separate. I bore the responsibility of making that call. Most shamefully, my unfulfilled need for intimacy triggered me to act.

Our discussions following that first encounter took many directions between how-did-it-happen and what-to-do-next. My argument: Scott stopped paying attention to himself and to me. His response: things weren't the same after Nick and his friends left for college. Our families drifted apart, and Scott didn't feel as involved with the smaller dance productions at the YMCA.

When I suggested his lack of interest in his career was a problem, he cited the downturn of the economy. He wasn't as resilient as I with my losses beginning with *Jubilee* on to the demise of Mikel's *Performing Arts Academy*. I loved the larger productions but helping children perform is precious no matter how many or how few students. Scott and I acknowledged our unhappiness but not which happened first, his dissolution with life in general or my sense of loneliness.

***

"Your dad and I decided to go our separate ways." I hated to break the news to Nick over the phone, but it had become his preferred method of communicating since going off to college.

Silence at the other end of the line. "I could have waited until we got together, but I didn't want you to hear it from someone other than me." More silence. "Even if Dad moves out of the house, we'll still be family, just not living together."

"Mom, I left home and we're still a family."

"Thanks for understanding." I shifted the subject to his job, girl-friend, and laundry. "I can send André to pick up your dirty clothes."

"Not necessary. I have access to washing machines at my apartment."

"I started dating someone."

"I assumed you had. What did Grams and André say?"

"Mom understands. She's been through this sort of separation years ago. We haven't told André yet. Your dad and I will break the news after school tonight."

"Good luck. Be ready for a tantrum."

"Thanks for understanding. I love you."

"I love you, too, Mom."

***

Scott had accepted the inevitable and contained his deep seated hurt and anger during our discussion with André at the kitchen table. Fortunately, Mom was in her room sorting through her things and brooding over the last batch of old magazines I disposed of.

André jumped up and yelled, "Dad, Mom's kicking you out of our house! Are you going to sit here and let that happen?"

I was prepared for my son's anger, but not the direct hit to my vulnerability. I shouldn't have been surprised. Scott had been the soft touch when André wanted something. I always saw to my boys' needs, but I tried to hold back their impulsive wish list. André played both parents to his advantage. Scott loves his boys and I admire—love him—for being such a special Dad. But, this time I was taking an unfair hit.

Scott calmed André as much as possible with assurances that we would remain a family, we would continue to support his athletic interests, and that Mom wasn't a mean ogre.

Scott's third point didn't register with my son, and I felt terrible. I needed my sister.

Caroline did a phone wince when I told her about Corky, but quickly understood how I felt.

Sis." Her pause for emphasis wasn't necessary. Any conversation starting with *Sis* got my attention. "It's about time you started tending to your needs. I'm sorry if your family is caught off guard and probably angry with you, but you have always given of yourself, often at a heavy emotional cost. Everyone takes advantage of your upbeat attitude, your indomitable spirit. With Mom, for instance, you go the extra mile. Cindy and I appreciate all you have done, but we don't often enough tell you. I am telling you now, don't ever beat yourself up for owning your needs and acting on them. If your family is feeling sorry for themselves, they will get over it."

I humbly agreed with my sister's observation and I allowed a bit of anger to surface, mostly at myself for denying my feelings. I am upbeat by nature, but not all lemons can be turned into lemonade, at least not right away. André will eventually understand that he isn't the only person I want to love with all my heart. Scott will rise above his anger and actually believe what he has graciously been telling our sons about our separation. Mom will continue to be my mother, justifiably self-centered after her lifetime of giving. Nicholas is free to pursue his love interests knowing the depth of my love for him.

 CHAPTER 36

Bringing Mom back from the emergency room, a heavy silence persisted in the car.

"Why are we stopping here?"

More games, Mom? "This is our house."

"I don't think so." She shook her head with such determination, I became concerned.

"Mom, this has been your home for the past six years."

"Not this house."

"The pain medicine must have you confused." I struggled to get her from the passenger seat onto her wheelchair. "Once inside, you'll recognize your things."

"Are you and Scott planning to buy this house? I liked our America West homes."

"Caroline and Cindy own both our old houses as rentals. You were with me when I decided to buy out here."

"For you and Scott and your boys. I have my own place."

"Yes, and this is it. Your home is here, with André and me." I wheeled her through the family room and into the kitchen. "Are you hungry?"

"They brought lunch before... Where was I?"

"Mountainview Hospital." An inquisitive expression locked onto her face. "You fell and those cute paramedics took you to the emergency room." If anything, she should recall flirting with them while arguing with me about who should carry her purse.

"Hospital?"

"You went to the emergency room. Thought you broke your ankle."

"I didn't break my hip, did I? My life's over if I did."

"It was only a slight fracture, not even requiring a cast."

"Are you sure I didn't break my leg. It really hurts."

"The doctor sent pain medication home with you. It's in your purse." I checked my watch. "If it hurts bad, he said you can take another one in an hour."

"I better take one now. Then I should lie down."

"The doctor said every four hours."

"When he breaks his leg, he can wait four hours. This is my broken leg." She glanced around the room. "And my house." She attempted to stand. "Ouch. Give me that pill, and push me into *my* bedroom."

Mom, back to her old self, felt comforting. Prepared for bed and tucked under the sheets, I brought her a pill and a glass of water.

"Come and lie down next to me like Caroline."

I pulled the chair closer. "I'll sit here until you fall asleep, Mommie." A blank stare, as if she hadn't heard, or perhaps confused me with my sister. Caroline and I had made a game out of calling Betty Jeanne *Mommie* like two little girls vying for attention. She protested, but we knew she loved it.

She arched her eyebrows sensing something was wrong. "Where are Scott and your boys?"

Oh, oh. Had her mind settled two years back before Scott and I separated or even before Nick went off to college? "André is in school. Nick graduated and lives in an apartment with roommates."

"I know, but where is Scott?"

A genuine concern or a rub, I couldn't tell. "Do you remember Stephen Shultz back when I was in high school?"

"Yes, he was a nice young man. Always thought you should stay together."

"Well, we didn't. And I think you know why."

"Remind me why you two broke up."

A tinge of nostalgia, I stared off in the distance. "Our lives took us in different directions. Sometimes that happens to people even though they still love each other."

"Is that what happened with Scott?"

"Yes, *Mommie*, that's what happened between Scott and me, and yes, we still love each other and continue to raise our two sons."

"You said Nick moved away."

"He still needs both his parents like Caroline and I still need you and Dad."

"What about your new guy?"

I drew a deep breath and blinked back the flow of tears. "He doesn't live here any more."

"Can he come back? I liked him."

"Mom, I got too much going on right now to even think about it. You just broke your leg—"

"Only a slight fracture in my ankle." A wry smile. "Didn't even require a cast."

I ignored her attempt to mock me and continued, "Mornings I conduct my seniors' exercise classes, afternoons I rehearse the children's dance routines for their upcoming show, and I have my jobs at the YMCA." I didn't mention my recent private investigation work, because she and André go to bed before I leave the house.

"Don't forget about practicing for *Jubilee*."

"Mom, *Jubilee* was 25 years ago. The show I'm rehearsing is a Mistinguett production of *Showgirl Follies*. Jackie, my best friend, and Kimba from *Siegfried and Roy* are in it with me."

"That's nice. Will Nick and André take me to see it."

"Of course, they will." *Patience.* "You know I'm doing it just for you."

"I can't go if my hip breaks." She shook her head. "My life will be over when that happens."

"You won't break your hip, if you use your walker."

"I don't see too good and sometimes I forget things."

"Yes." *When convenient.*

A vacant stare. "I wanted to say something."

"You'll think of it when you wake up." Hopefully, the pill will kick in and she'll drop off to sleep.

A satisfied sigh as if solving a mystery. "Corky…" Eyelids closed and soft breaths escaped her lips.

***

Corky. A thrill reminiscent of our touching hands that night after the basketball tournament. I lingered at Mom's bedside, dwelling on the quiet afternoons Corky and I spent at his apartment listening to music, watching movies, munching popcorn, and playing chess. After friends and family adjusted to Scott's and my decision to live apart, the entire city became our playground. We'd tool around in his pickup truck rather than my car with *SHOWGRL* plates. Strolling through the parks, we'd suddenly become competitive and try to out-run each other. Being the same age with equal vitality had advantages. A sudden burst of energy could develop in an instant. From the parking lot, we'd race to the door of a restaurant or grocery store. Heading down separate sides of a glass enclosed area, we peeked between display pieces and made faces at each other. At the gym, Corky pumped iron, and I ran three and a half miles on the treadmill every day. We bowled, golfed, and attended André's games as well as some UNLV sports events. Our capacity for making love seemed endless.

We celebrated our first anniversary with dining at my favorite restaurant, Hugo's Cellar, at the Four Queens Casino. Back at my house to change into casual clothes, he paused under the archway to our bedroom and hesitated at the threshold.

"There is no mistletoe," I chuckled. "Christmas was four months ago." We had been in a giddy mood all day.

"I know. I have something to ask."

"We've been sharing this bedroom for these many months, and now you're playing *Captain, May I*." I beckoned him forward. "Yes, you may take three giant steps to collect your prize." I spread out my arms. "Me!"

He dropped to one knee like this was some kind of church.

I laughed and said, "Only Catholics genuflect before entering a holy place. Here you can walk right in and take off your clothes."

He recited, "I have nothing left, nothing to give you. I have no pride, no dignity, no money."

"That's okay, no matter what—"

"Let me finish." He squirmed, obviously in pain. "I don't even know how we will make a living, but I promise I'll love you the rest of your life."

"Are you proposing to me?"

"Yes, you silly girl. Now accept my offer so I can get up."

I stood in front of him. "Grab my shoulders and lift yourself." On his feet, I pulled his face to mine and kissed him passionately. Releasing him, I said, "Yes, I will marry you."

Seemingly, out of nowhere—from his pocket, I assumed—he pulled out a ring while I issued his kiss.

"It's beautiful." I slid it onto my finger and held it to the light from the afternoon sun through the French doors. "We have to go downstairs and show this to Mom."

I peeked into her bedroom and said. "Come see what Corky just gave me." I waited with my hands behind my back.

She approached and said, "Now, what's so important."

I held out my hand. "What do you think of this?"

From its chain around her neck, she raised her illuminated magnifying lens to her eye. "Very nice." She glanced at Corky who stood proudly at my side. "Where's mine?" Typical Mom.

"You had your chance. This is my ring and he is my man." We shared a giggle.

Corky called his brothers, John and Ron, and his sister, Cathy. He recited the same lines he used on me before offering the ring.

I said, "By the way, Shakespeare, since when have you taken up poetry?"

"That was Kurt Russell's proposal to his dancer girlfriend in the movie *Tombstone*? John recognized it right away."

"Isn't that cute. I bet Wyatt Earp wore his marshal's star when he asked *his* showgirl to marry him."

Corky pulled the box of Copenhagen snuff from his hip pocket where it had worn a permanent circular imprint in the fabric, and flashed the metal cover like a badge. "I'm a detective and if you refuse to marry me…"

The memory triggered a burst of laughter that snorted through my nose by trying to stifle it. My emotions seesawing, I began to sob. The sheet covering my mother's small form gently lifted with each breath. Through blurry eyes, I studied her face, its beauty radiating. She didn't need to be reminded of all the turmoil when Corky lived with us. André accepted his dad living at our friend's rental house, but resented Corky—or any man I might have chosen—taking his dad's place. When tempers exploded, Corky had to leave.

Ready to tiptoe from Mom's bedside, my emotions took control of my voice. *"Mommie,* what should I do?"

Eyes closed, she whispered, "Listen to your heart, Mikel."

***

My first priority has always been my sons, and with Nick graduating and moving on with his life, my attention focused on André. If I lost either of my sons' respect, I accept responsibility, but I will never stop loving them. They are an actual part of me, my blood running through their veins. As my mother's in mine? Are my sons me? Am I my mother? Of course not. The umbilical cords were severed at birth. We are free of each other bound only by unconditional love.

After my boys' happiness, my next priority is to make sure that I live my life to its fullest, not unhappy and agitated like my mother, growing old and dying without being in love. I need someone to love me and keep me safe. Only then will my future be a fun journey where I welcome with open arms and an open heart my children, grandchildren if God grants me any, and an intimate relationship.

I want to enter the next phase of my life with enthusiasm and the spirit of adventure until my jet engines flame out, and I skydive into my next mysterious existence.

Listen to your heart, Mikel, a mother's advice.

CHAPTER 37

I hesitated in the YMCA parking lot to contain my emotions before starting my dance class. Had I made the right choice to leave Mom with Scott and my boys at her deathbed? Did she want me out of the room so she could leave? Die? Lisa, her hospice therapist, seemed to think so. *One hour*, Mom. Hang in there for another hour.

I considered my students and parents waiting for me to begin class. Children can sense when adults are experiencing problems, and it is best to be honest with them. *God is coming to take my Mommie to heaven, and I hope He will give me one more chance to tell her how much I love her.* Armed with the proper words to tell my students—and to satisfy the chaos in my head—I smiled and it felt genuine.

Returning to hospice, Nick met me at the door. "Grandma's gone. I held her hand when she took her last breath eight minutes ago. "

EPILOGUE

Sitting here with my eyes closed, I can visualize your face taste-fully made up, hair tinted blond, wearing your gray suit with a ruffled blouse that you had chosen. The pink fleece slippers are from André, but I've already mentioned his Christmas gift that you didn't get to open. I know you understand his sensitive nature and that he couldn't stand to see his Grams die. He cried his eyes out at your memorial service and misses you more each day.

At class this afternoon, one little sweetheart asked, "Did your mother go to see Auntie Caroline in Ohio?" I had explained you were on your way to heaven, but for a five-year-old, Auntie Caroline in Ohio is an easier concept to grasp. I consider the students in my classes as my children, so Caroline would be their auntie and you would be their grandma.

It's quite dark, the December sun dropped behind the moun-tains even before I left class, and a streak of clouds along the horizon is blocking the moon. I can barely distinguish our side-by-side crypts, yours and mine. Patience while I live out the rest of my life before joining you. God allowed Betty Jeanne Peterson a full life of nearly ninety adventure-filled years. Maybe God will grant me another fifty. I don't need to outlive you, but I want my life to end differently. We already talked about that.

Your passing was beautifully sad. Nick stayed at your side, holding your hand as you began your journey. You held on long enough for me to finish my dance class, but couldn't wait until I returned to your room. You knew I couldn't stand to watch you leave. Eight minutes late! I created a shameful tantrum while aides struggled to wheel you out of the room on a gurney. Nick restrained and comforted me.

Caroline wrote your obituary, and it read like *Whose Who of Albuquerque*, six kids and as many grand children. (She didn't include my dance students.) I'll let you know when I become a grandma. If Nick dates a girl you'd like him to marry, nudge him in her direction. Nick, not André! Must get number two son through high school and college first.

Almost everybody bunked at our house the night before your funeral. Caroline wanted to sleep in your bed, but her feet would stick out. She and Cindy slept with me in my king size. The constant stream of florist deliveries, the catering trucks, and the cars packed with friends expressing condolences must have piqued the neighbors' curiosity, and the string of limousines lined up the next morning confirmed their suspicions that a mob family lived next door. I like that image. *The Albuquerque Clan*. Had a passer-by peeked in after our entourage left, he would have mistaken our home for a florist shop.

Caroline donated some of the arrangements before I could stop her, but I salvaged the most of them. Don't know what I'll do with all the vases, but I have petals drying to blend into potpourri with a touch of your sachet. Your aroma will continue into the future, maybe freshened with a dab of your Liz Taylor Perfume from time to time.

At Palm Mortuary, we began our celebration of your life. Each of us told stories about the good old days. We cried, then smiled, then laughed. Caroline did a spoof of Texas Papa's little ladies whipping up a batch of cookie dough with a bowl and wooden spoon. What a hoot. Gary chuckled, but I knew my older brother was hurting, as were Pam and Suzanne. Bringing us kids closer together as a family was your last little gift to us.

Nick told the most stories from those years he slept in the bunk bed above yours, and I thought you guys were asleep. André remembered an incident back when he was five or six that bonded you two forever. He had broken my little Spanish fountain boy, and you covered for him.

My shared memories jumped from the turkey I won in grade school for our thanksgiving table to your coming to my last performance as a showgirl in *Sassy*. Just for you, Mommie. Through tears and giggles, I realized how much I needed to please you. I know you never stopped being proud of me, even when some of my decisions weren't very praiseworthy.

You would have been excited to see your five kids whooping and hollering with the limo windows down and the rooftop slid open, heading down Las Vegas Boulevard to your new home. Kind of like *Helldorado Days* when André, Scott, and I led the parade in my Thunderbird convertible. Unfortunately, this time our police escort didn't blast its sirens. I'll oblige families like us when my new law enforcement career gets off the ground.

I'm sure our brother Jeff and baby Sharon Jane rode with us, but you can ask them for yourself. And, of course, Peggy and Don, your brother and sister. I heard you talking to them when you hardly knew who I was. It didn't offend me because you had future business with them. I hope they paved the way for you, as I am sure Jeff and baby Sharon Jane did.

On the way to your new home, we watched you fly off toward heaven, the cloud formation of letters 'B' and 'J' in reverse. I keep watching the sky for more messages, because you were the first female pilot in Albuquerque. That piece of cloth at the foot of your casket, along with your make-up kit, is a swatch from the tail they cut off your shirt the day you soloed. I asked the funeral director to put your stuff down by your feet, and I peeked to see that he had complied. I didn't tell anyone because my family would laugh at me, but I knew you wouldn't. We were so much alike, and now I am you continuing your life through my eyes.

Caroline received your message the day she returned to her clinic. Having a Betty Jeanne Peterson bump her way into Caroline's busy schedule was classic! I hope you sent a woman with your name rather than a spirit, because Caroline doesn't believe in ghosts like you and I do. I know you loved both of us, Caroline just a bit more. I understand. I am not jealous. My sister did everything right. College and a career to make you proud. I had to do everything the hard way, yet always landed on my feet. I'm a bit more like you than my sister is. You gave Dad two girls and my gift to you, Betty Jeanne Peterson, are my two boys.

The day the hospital moved you to hospice, a bird from a cluster of three broke formation and headed toward Nathan Adelson while the other two veered in the direction of Palm Mortuary where Caroline and I were heading to make arrangements. I'm not sure what you were wanting to tell us, but don't stop giving signs.

You told me to follow my heart regarding relationships, but what about my career? I came out of retirement and danced one last performance in *Showgirl Follies*. I did it for you, and it revived my need to entertain. I love teaching my students, watching them develop their stage presence, but it doesn't satisfy my desire to excite an audience. Is there hope for me?

Brightening the sky makes me feel better, but I need a sign more definite than the moon breaking free of the clouds. I have all night. I can wait.

A shooting star! I got it. Thanks, Mom. I love you.

***

The grass felt cold on my back, but I could hardly keep up with wishes as stars began shooting across the sky. Before I went to bed, I woke up Caroline to tell her about my experience. After reminding me that Dayton is three hours ahead of Las Vegas time, she explained that media showers occur on a regular basis. In December they are called *Geminids*. Fancy name or not, Mom had announced, *Mikel's life of stardom continues.*

***

Obituary submitted by her daughter, Dr. Caroline Peterson

Betty Jean Peterson passed away on December 8, 2014 at the age of 89. Visitation will be held at Palm Mortuary located at 6701 North Jones Blvd on Sunday, December 14 from 4-7 pm. Services honoring B.J. will be held on Monday, December 15 at 12:00 noon, in the Palm Mortuary Chapel. B.J. was preceded in death by her daughter Sharon Jane, by her son Jeffrey Peterson, by her sister Peggy Atchison and by her brother Don Baker. She is survived by her children, Gary Peterson and his wife Sue Ann Peterson of Houston, Texas, Pamela Peterson of Albuquerque, New Mexico; Suzanne Peterson of Phoenix, Arizona; Dr. Caroline Peterson and partner Cindy Schaffer of Dayton, Ohio, and Mikel Peterson and Scott Meiers of Las Vegas, Nevada. She is also survived by six grandchildren, Sterling Czar and wife Devon, of Breckenridge, Colorado; Jayme Czar Parker and Justin Czar both of Albuquerque, New Mexico; Candace Battafarano and husband Phillip of Phoenix, Arizona; Nicholas and André Meiers, both of Las Vegas

Nevada. B.J. was also blessed with seven great-grand children, Hayden Caldes and Hudson and Mia Grace Parker of Albuquerque, New Mexico; Nico and Sophia Battafarano of Phoenix, Arizona; and Braylynn Elizabeth and Dalton Sterling of Breckenridge, Colorado. B.J. is survived by her cousin, Doris Sullivan and many nieces and nephews who she beloved and felt it was important to keep connected with her own children.

Betty Jeanne was born May 18th, 1925 in Quanah, Texas. She graduated from Quanah High School at the age of 16 and lost her high school sweetheart December 7, 1941 in Pearl Harbor. She attended Texas Women's University in Denton, Texas. During World War II, she frequently visited her father, Sterling Barker, at his construction sites of the U.S. Army in Colorado, New Mexico, and Texas. On one of these travels, she met Dr. Joseph Peterson of Albuquerque, New Mexico, whom she married and had five children with. Their introduction was a malt shop and their first date was diverted to the delivery of a baby in rural, New Mexico where Betty assisted in the delivery. Soon thereafter, her father Sterling built the first Osteopathic Hospital in the state of New Mexico, in Belen, which was later moved to Albuquerque. She and Dr. Peterson ran the hospital, where Betty served in Radiology and as a Surgical Assistant. Betty was President of the Doctors' Wives Association for several years, raising revenue to develop scholarships for medical students and supporting young physician going into practice. One to two times a year she and Joe would fly their private plane into Mexico to drop off medical supplies and deliver care to the underserved. This is where Betty took a love for flying and became the first woman to solo an airplane in the state of New Mexico. In 1954, she and Joe divorced. She then met Don Lesmen Chavez and had two children. She spent the next 20 years in Albuquerque raising her two girls, taking them to cross country and track meets around the region. After her two daughters were raised, she turned the focus to her grandchildren. She ultimately moved to Las Vegas, Nevada, to be closer to her youngest grandchildren. Because B.J. had a "gift of gab", she knew no strangers. She was the "air traffic controller" of stories and current affairs in the family. Most of all, she befriended all she met, Loved all she met and gave advice to all she met, with the intent to make their life experience better.

AUTHOR'S NOTES

During a 2014 Fourth of July yard party, our host introduced Mikel as a former *Jubilee* Showgirl and two-time Olympic performer and Roger as a *famous* author. We struck up a conversation about the mob culture of old Las Vegas. When she asked about my writing, I described my most recent project, *PRIVATE RICHARD LESLIE*, a memoir of my father-in-law who parachuted onto Corregidor Island during the battle of Manila in WWII.

She said, "My mother deserves something like that."

She approached me during the fireworks display—a year later—and said, "I want you to write a story about my mother."

Anyone who would continue a conversation after a year's interruption captured my attention. I said, "Your memoir as a showgirl would be more interesting."

"That's what Mom said before she died last December."

"I'm sorry for your family's loss. Are you prepared to take your mother's advice?"

"Only if Mom and my sister, Caroline, get the credit they deserve."

I added, "And, only if you share the authorship. I don't do ghost writing."

"Agreed. If I'm to be your partner, we go fifty/fifty on everything."

I extended my hand.

She grasp it and leaned forward. "In my culture, we seal agreements with a kiss.

I held my grip. "In my culture we shake hands." Recalling last year's mob conversation, I added, "The mingling of blood not necessary."

We shook hands and touched lips. Neither asked to sign a contract.

Roger Storkamp's previous published works include *Private Richard Leslie; a Memoir, Light Years from Home,* and his trilogy: *Thelma's Quilt, 'Neath a Crescent Moon,* and *Miss West,* the saga of two families set in Bovine, Minnesota, a fictional town where real people live. A town without a zip code.

available at:
Books and Birch
3016 Haddon Drive
Las Vegas, NV 89134
(702) 228-1477

Mikel and Roger wish to acknowledge the following:

Laurie Storkamp who offered support and, with her friend, Victoria Coombs, read and re-read each chapter for clarity.

Joyce Newman, fellow Minnesotan, who performed the final line edit.

Daniel Storkamp who touched up and formatted the pictures from Mikel's photo album.

Mikel's sons Nicholas and André for their tacit support.

Scott Meiers for the cover design.

Hundreds of Mikel's present and former students whose lives she touched.